# Newlove

## At the Centre of Rugby League

# Paul Newlove

## with Andrew Quirke

*LONDON LEAGUE PUBLICATIONS Ltd*

# Newlove
## At the Centre of Rugby League

A CIP catalogue record for this book is available from the British Library.

First published in Great Britain in November 2004 by:
London League Publications Ltd, P.O. Box 10441, London E14 8WR

ISBN:                        1-903659-19-1

Cover design by:             Stephen McCarthy Graphic Design
                             46, Clarence Road, London N15 5BB

Layout:                      Peter Lush

Printed and bound by:   Biddles Ltd, Kings Lynn

# Foreword

World class is a phrase used quite often in sport – as everyone knows, this relates to an individual's ability to compete at the very highest level of international competition and thrive in this environment. To have an unassuming world class athlete is a very rare commodity indeed, if not completely obsolete in these days of ultra confident people.

Paul Newlove fits into both of the above categories with ease; he carried the mantle of a world class player into many big games on both the domestic and international stage and rarely failed to reach the high standards everyone expected of him. One of Paul's most endearing qualities was his modesty, he genuinely believed he didn't belong with the high profile players who he rubbed shoulders with at international level and he struggled to accept his rapid elevation to the international rugby league stage.

Nevertheless, from Featherstone, he moved first to Bradford and then to St Helens and eventually looked comfortable in what was an outstanding period of success at the St Helens club. I was both fortunate and unfortunate to play with and against Paul through several stages of his career. All the coaches who previewed the threat posed by 'Newy' truly respected his danger to their side. He was one of the few players coaches breathed a sign of relief when he was brought to the ground.

I know Paul will be disappointed his playing days came to an end in the manner that they did, but he can hold his head high for the way he produced time after time at all levels.

Off the field, Paul was drier than a white wine and my time rooming with him on the 1992 tour will long live in some of my better memories of rugby league.

I hope this book fully reflects the exploits of a quality bloke who has been one of Great Britain's best performers in recent times.

## Daryl Powell

Daryl Powell had a distinguished rugby league career with Sheffield Eagles, Leeds Rhinos, Keighley Cougars and Great Britain. He is currently director of football at Leeds Rhinos.

### Thank you from Andrew Quirke
Especially to Niccy Shiel. For producing the book to: Peter Lush, Dave Farrar, Huw Richards, Steve McCarthy, Bernard Platt, David Williams, Mike Critchley, Richard Luck, Kevin Gill, and the staff at Biddles Ltd. For participating in interviews to: John Newlove, Margaret Newlove, Adele Newlove, Paul Wellens, Peter Fox, Freddie Levine, John Hill, Sean Long, Chris Joynt, Carl Hall, Mal Kay, Claire Mannion, Paul Bennett, Daryl Powell and Deryck Fox. For providing support to: Marian Quirke, Graham Wilson, Chris Gill, Mike Gill, Paul Gill, Melissa Hackney, Ste Barker, Tania Costello-Parr, Al Ferrier, Colin and Helen, Rochelle Brown, Andy Heaton, Deanne McGlinn, Ben and Jules, Chris Lawrence, Doug Laughton, Ruth Sephton, Richard Luck and Paul Bennett.

# Preface

Paul Newlove was one of the best players of his generation. He is in the all-time top 20 English try scorers. An exciting player who every time the ball came his way, his team's supporters held their breath as they knew something could happen. Similarly, a player who by being tackled, normally a simple act in the game, would provoke cheers from relieved opposition supporters.

He was a powerful centre who could score long range tries with surprising pace for a big man. He was a winger's dream who could be seemingly wrapped up by opposition defenders yet was still able to flick out a miracle ball round the backs of his tacklers. A master at creating space for the player outside him as Anthony Sullivan would testify.

He started his career at his local club Featherstone before a big money move to Bradford and then he became the world's most expensive rugby league player with a move to St Helens. That move saw him stay at the club for eight years, one in the eye for those who said he wouldn't settle away from Yorkshire. People at the club say he was a consummate professional. Despite a 130 miles round-trip everyday, he was rarely late for training.

A record breaker in rugby league, he remains Great Britain's youngest ever international and holds try scoring records aplenty. He has won four Super League titles, three Challenge Cup winners' medals and a World Club Championship, a player recognised as 'the final piece in the jigsaw' of the all-conquering St Helens side of the summer era. When his signing was announced, St Helens fans were delighted as he had been one of the stars of the 1995 World Cup for England. It was a sign that things were about to change as he was the first big name player that Saints had managed to snare before Wigan did. A move symbolic of Saints future trophy winning successes ahead of their arch rivals.

He is also an enigma within the sport; a shy and private man who rarely gave interviews, and didn't go in for big displays of emotion while on the field.

Now retired, with his status as a legend in the game secure; the question from rugby league followers remains: "What's Newy really like?" Here is Paul Newlove's own story. A reflection of the man himself, it is an honest account infused with a dry sense of humour.

## Andrew Quirke

Andrew Quirke is a St Helens RLFC supporter who edited various Saints fanzines and websites for eight years. His first book *Knowsley Road* was published in 2001, two years later Andrew co-wrote rugby league legend Doug Laughton's autobiography *A Dream Come True*. Andrew currently contributes the 'A Quirky view' column to Saints official matchday programme. He enjoyed writing this book with Paul and there were a few good laughs. None more so than the first time Paul saw Andrew's car - the Charabang.

# Contents

Playing for Featherstone
(Photo: David Williams)

# 1. Early doors

I was born on 10 August 1971 on the settee in my parents' semi-detached house on Cobblers Lane in Pontefract into what can only be described as a rugby league family. All the men in my immediate family have played for Featherstone Rovers. I have two brothers, Sean who is a year older than me and Richard who is seven years younger than me. I played alongside Sean at Featherstone, I signed first then he joined a year or so after me. We did actually play together in the same team for Rovers, in one game we were a centre and wing partnership. Sean's career was ended by a badly broken leg when he played in the 'A' team for Featherstone against Hull. He finished playing after that. It's a shame because he could have made it, he was quick, a similar build to me and had a rugby head on him. There wasn't much between us really. Sean never really played much amateur rugby league. He went to Jubilee, a local amateur side. I think he only played two games, one of which was at Post Office Road in a final and he scored a couple of tries. After that game the cry went up from the Featherstone board: 'Right, we want another Newlove!' So Sean was signed after two games of rugby league. He could always play the game, I knew that, but he had never played long term. He had never seemed that bothered, he'd always played football as a kid.

Richard has always played rugby and he too signed for Featherstone in March 1995, then he had a spell at Wakefield and is back at Featherstone now. Of course, my dad John played, he was captain for Featherstone at Wembley in the 1973 and 1974 Challenge Cup finals, and then later joined Hull. I went to watch my dad at Wembley play for Hull against Hull KR in 1980, they lost and that turned out to be his last game.

Then there is my uncle Charlie Stone, my mum's brother who played at Featherstone with my dad and for Hull and Bradford. I went back to Wembley in 1983 to see him play for Hull when they lost against Featherstone. I'll never forget it because he head butted Pete Smith near the sticks. Hull had been winning 12-5 with 20 minutes left, but Rovers fought back to level the scores. Steve Quinn kicked the goal and that was it, my uncle Charlie had head butted Featherstone to a famous cup win. We ripped into him after the game. We said he might as well have worn a blue and white

1

shirt and that all he had to do was tackle Pete Smith. We were Hull supporters then as Charlie was playing there.

The family wasn't a rugby league obsessed one though. As a youngster I never really went to watch my dad regularly. Occasionally I would go, but I didn't like it as it was freezing cold, so they would leave me at home. Given the choice of being stood at Post Office Road on a wintry afternoon or staying at my Nan's watching *The Muppet Show* on a Sunday teatime, the Muppets won every time. I was never really into watching rugby league or any sport for that matter as a youngster. I've always played sport, whatever sport I took up I could do it. Some kids can't, they're better at other stuff. I was one of those kids who could play rugby, football, cricket, tennis, you name it. I'll have a go at any sport.

I started playing rugby when I was really young. I was a stand off. At that age, we didn't really have positions, it was just a case of picking the ball up and running with it. They probably put me at stand off because that's where my dad played. I can't remember passing it much.

Growing up, I was never really an out-and-out Featherstone supporter. I would go the odd game with my mates who were supporters. Also, my dad played there. It was always in the back of my head that I might follow him there. My dad never pushed any of us into playing. He is laid back. He doesn't say much, maybe I'm a bit like him. He used to play with us in the garden though. I also remember he used to take me and Sean down to Post Office Road with him when he was going to see Freddie the groundsman.

Sean and I used to play on the big field with a rugby ball. My dad used to run about with us and play touch-and-pass behind the sticks as the dead ball area was the width of 'our' pitch. We used to try and kick goals on there as well. We were only tiny and to have all that space was great, the pitch seemed massive. My dad never coached us though, he left us to it. It's different if your dad is a professional rugby player, there's an expectation that you will play and people say 'if you're as good as your dad you'll be a good 'un'. My dad and I were different styles though. I'm a bit bigger than he was. He started off on the wing, then went to centre, then went to stand off when his coach Peter Fox moved him there. That's when my dad's career really took off. He played well at centre but I think he enjoyed it more at stand off and got more opportunities setting tries up. Whereas I've always been a runner, a finisher and someone who scores tries. In any event, I think I've come up to the expectations.

I went to Cobblers Lane Primary School, just over the road from where we lived. It was great, I only had to leave home at five to nine to get to school. There was no rugby league team, so I played football for them.

I wasn't very interested in school and I left with no qualifications. I wasn't the brightest spark at school work. I remember getting shouted at and kicked out of the classroom from time to time and got up to mischief like everybody else. I never did anything really bad though to warrant being expelled or anything like that. I couldn't wait to get out of school, not that I knew what I wanted to do when I left though. I'd always played rugby and maybe that was my get out. Looking back, after all I have achieved in rugby, I will always be very grateful for it.

The secondary school I went to was Pontefract Park High School and I played stand off for their union side as they didn't have a rugby league side. I got a rollicking off the teacher as I played union the way they play it now, lots of kicking. They wanted the ball to be put through the hands. It just doesn't work in union. I refused to play that way and kept kicking it all the time. He said he would bring me off if I didn't play to his style but I went my own way and thought 'balls to him'.

I was good at football and when I was about 13, played for Ferrybridge because my dad worked there at the power station. Sean and I played in the same team. Sean was good; a goal-scoring centre forward and I played in midfield or on the left wing, as I was quick enough to play out wide. I had a trial for York City, I thought I'd done well but obviously not well enough as they didn't sign me. They wrote to me and said: "Due to the high standard required our Youth Policy permits only a limited number of vacancies each year. Unfortunately you have not been selected for further trials".

Then a scout came from Sheffield Wednesday to watch me; I don't know who had put my name forward for that. He looked at me one day and at the end of the game he came over and said that I had to concentrate on stopping the ball and looking up, when I could do that I should give him a ring. I never rung him back, I just thought 'let's pick the ball up and run with it, let's play rugby now'.

3

One of my heroes is Pelé, I really admired him. When the football World Cup comes round and the old footage of him is on television, it's great. I love watching the moment from 1970 where the goalkeeper comes out to get the ball, Pelé dummies and then runs round to have a shot. He didn't score, but it was amazing skill. To think of a move like that is genius. I wish he had scored. The other wonderful moment is where he had a shot from the halfway line. Again he didn't score, but for him to see the goalkeeper off his line and try it from such distance is incredible.

I can't watch a football match now. I'll sometimes watch highlights, but that's about it, I don't really watch sport. I just don't find it interesting, if I'm not playing rugby league, I don't watch it. That might seem like an awful thing to say, but I don't think it is; it's just the way I am. People find this strange. I've played rugby league for Great Britain and all that, yet when they ask me: 'Are you watching the game?' I just say: 'What game? What's on?' Of course, then I get 'bloody hell Newy, you're laid back'. I've had the laid back comment all through my career. If that's what people think, that's up to them, but I don't think I am laid back. Maybe I just don't show as much emotion as other people, maybe I'm just cool under pressure.

I had started playing rugby league in the under-9 team for Travellers Saints. The coaches were Alan Agar, who was playing for Hull KR at the time, and Vince Farrar. There were some good coaches down at Travellers and they were all locals. Charlie Birdsall was there, a Hull back rower, but from Featherstone. Terry Ramshaw was another of the coaches. I became aware when I was playing in the under-15s that there was a bit of fuss about me. I would sometimes get a whisper that a scout might be coming to look at me. Of course, I didn't know who they were.

When I ran out to play, I'd look around and think: 'He could be the scout, he looks like a scout, he's stood there on his own and he's never been to the games before'. It made me a bit nervous and I would end up trying too hard. I would start chasing the game, trying to impress and do nothing as a result. It's just human nature because I wanted to do well.

I remember in my professional career, in one game I needed two more tries to break a record at Featherstone. In the first half I ran all over the field to get the two tries and nothing was happening for me. At half time I was told to relax and play my own game. I came out for the second half, waited for the ball to come to me and I got the tries.

Anyway, I came up through the ranks, then all of a sudden when I was 14-years-old, I stopped playing. I had to jump age groups and it would have meant me playing against lads the year above me. I didn't want to do that so went off to play football instead until I caught up and then I came back. Then I played for Featherstone Miners Welfare who are based just behind Rovers' ground in Post Office Road.

The coach there was Pete Smith, the man my uncle Charlie had head butted at Wembley. Pete was the main influence on me turning professional. From the age of 15 until reaching signing on age is when young players learn a lot about the game. It's nice playing when as a kid, but I didn't really know what I was doing.

Pete coached alongside the legendary Cyril Kellett, who holds the record for most conversions (8) in a Wembley Challenge Cup Final. Iestyn Harris equalled the record in the 1999 Final. Pete brought a lot of ideas to the set up. We had a really good side - we were the main team in the village.

When the time came that we could sign as professionals, five or six out of that team signed. Only I went on further in the game. This surprised me because of the ability in that side and the youngsters who were there, I thought they were going to make it.

I don't know why some players make it and some don't. With some, they don't develop further, they don't grow. I wasn't the biggest kid, but then all of a sudden I grew. Some kids grow to their full potential when they are aged 15 or 16. I remember one kid who was meant to be a world beater; scouts came from everywhere to look at him. He was over six foot tall and of course everyone he was playing against at the time was smaller than him. He was swatting kids off left, right and centre. He got into the professional game and was never heard of again. He was alright against smaller kids, but once he faced blokes the same size as him, he couldn't do it. A young player must take that next step to become a professional, the game becomes quicker.

I could have gone to any number of sides when I turned professional, Featherstone was an attraction because it was so nearby. I was meant to sign for Leeds before Rovers came in for me. We were supposed to have a meeting with them. We went to Headingley, there was no-one there and everywhere was locked up. We finally found the groundsman and asked where everyone was, we were informed they'd gone on holiday. No one had turned up to meet us so my dad said: 'You're not going here'. One of the biggest clubs in rugby league and they hadn't turned up. I was going to sign for Hull, Brian Smith came to our house and they put me a deal together and I told my dad I would sign for them. They were my dad's last club as well, which was a good reason for me to go there. He said that was fine.

Along came Bob Ashby, who was the main financial backer at Featherstone. He knew my dad as he had played at the amateur club Ackworth when my dad played there. Bob rang my dad on a Saturday morning and asked what my plans were; my dad told him that I wanted to sign for Hull. He told my dad not to let me sign anything as he was going to come down to see me straight away. He came down, wrote me a cheque and asked if that beat Hull. I looked at it, looked at my dad and said: 'I'll sign for Featherstone dad, it's only down the road'. I think money talked. I signed for them on 23 July 1988 and I'm glad I did.

There isn't much to do in Featherstone, it was a mining village and now the pits have gone. When I played for Featherstone Rovers, they had some brilliant crowds. When we were in Division One we would often get four or five thousand. The ground didn't hold much more than that and when it was full, it had a great atmosphere. In terms of percentage of local population, they had really good crowds.

Rugby league is important to Featherstone. It's a big part of people's lives. There are people who have supported the club all their lives, then their kids do the same, that's how loyal they are. Their passion sometimes gets a bit out of hand, but I'll talk about that later.

There are the amateur clubs like Lions and Miners Welfare; which act as filter clubs for Rovers. Everyone plays rugby; it's always been a good catchment area for youngsters. These days though, the best young players don't really want to start at Featherstone and I can't ever see them getting into Super League. But I have some good memories of my time there.

**John and Margaret Newlove are Paul's parents.**

*John:* "Paul wasn't a lazy lad, he was always off running about as a youngster. He might have been lazy in the classroom though. I remember once he was playing rugby outside, it was getting dark and he ran straight into a fence while scoring a try. It gave him two black eyes."

When people ask me how soon it was when I thought Paul was something special, I answer 'straight away'. I have seen a lot of brilliant players and straight away I could tell that Paul had ability.

I didn't teach him things like sidesteps when he was growing up, he was just naturally gifted. I would show him how to pass in the garden though. I remember once watching him train at Featherstone under-13s and they were playing 'British Bulldog'. Paul was called out, he went one way the lad went the other and Paul was away.

He once played in two cup finals on the same day. He played rugby league for Featherstone Miners in the morning. Before the game, I said to the coach Pete Smith that if they were winning easily, could he take Paul off as he had a football final for Ferrybridge that afternoon. They were winning easily so he fetched Paul off. We headed down the motorway and got to the football final for the second half. They won that one as well.

Initially his main asset was his speed. As he progressed through his career, he lost that bit of speed but gained in strength.

Paul had a lot of success in his career but I think my proudest moment watching him was when England beat Australia at Wembley and he scored his famous interception try. We don't get many victories against the Aussies so that was one to savour. I would have loved to him to have been part of an Ashes winning Great Britain side but it wasn't to be."

*Margaret:* "There were loads of times I was worried about Paul getting hurt playing rugby. I remember him getting knocked out while playing for Featherstone against Leeds. I was told he was concussed. I went down and got in the ambulance with him. I thought 'when he comes round he'll go mad at me' but he didn't. His dad followed us in one car, Adele came in another. We were like the Boswells in the hospital. Having said that, I used to enjoy watching him play."

John Newlove had a distinguished rugby league career, including captaining Featherstone Rovers in their historic 1973 Wembley Challenge Cup Final victory. He returned to Wembley with Featherstone in 1974, but despite John scoring a try, they lost to Warrington. He played in four Yorkshire Cup Finals, and in 1976-77, his testimonial season, won the championship with Featherstone. He finished his career at Hull, including another Challenge Cup Final appearance in 1980.

With my older brother Sean:
Top right: Playing football at home
Top left: With the Challenge Cup won by Featherstone in 1973
Bottom left: Teenagers – playing football again
(Photos: Courtesy Newlove family)
Bottom right: My brother Richard playing for Featherstone
(Photo: David Williams)

# 2. Porter Paul at Featherstone

For my first few training sessions at Featherstone, I had to get the bus there as I was too young to drive. I was the new kid at the club so I didn't say much, but just went into the 'A' team dressing room. I played five 'A' team games before being brought into the first team. Being so young, it was quite intimidating going into the first team dressing room; everyone looked at me. I didn't say much, what could I say? They were professional players; many of them had been there for years and there I was, a young kid starting out. I let my playing do the talking, then I got into it and people opened up to me. They saw what I could do and I became part of it.

I didn't know Peter Fox before I signed for the club; my dad did through playing for him. Foxy's been a huge influence on me as a player and a person. I find it hard to describe. He gave me my chance at Featherstone and always stuck by me. Foxy has always been a straight talker, whatever he says, you can trust him. Some players didn't like him because he told them things straight and they didn't like that. He's told me things straight sometimes but I've always respected that.

My first proper game was a friendly against Dewsbury at Crown Flatt. I was a substitute and came on to play on the wing. I scored a 60-yard try going down the touchline. The pitch was like a rollercoaster, it went up and down that much. I beat the cover and went round to the sticks, it was a good try, plus I got £10 for winning the game. It was the first time I was paid to play rugby. £10 - I was made up.

Peter Fox put me on the wing at first just to keep me out of the way as I was a kid playing against men. My full debut was a Yorkshire Cup tie at Hull on 27 September 1988 where Featherstone lost 18-0 and I played on the wing. I got a few slaps on the back before I went on with people wishing me good luck. I remember that it was a very cold night. It wasn't misty but there was a bit of a haze in the air. I didn't really do anything, but made one break. I held my own and didn't look out of place.

I say that because I stayed in the first team. I didn't really notice much of a difference between the 'A' team and first team in terms of the pace of the games. I suppose I adjusted. Someone asked me about the difference and I said I could handle it, they replied that was because I had the ability to do it, whereas other people might find it a struggle to take that step up. The other step up where I have found the pace really quick is where you are playing international rugby against Australia. Some Super League games against the top sides can sometimes feel a bit like that too.

Five days after the Hull game, I scored my first points for Featherstone in a league match when I kicked four goals against Bradford Northern at Post Office Road. We lost 20-48.

Another early game I played on the wing was against Warrington's Des Drummond. It was a bit scary to be honest; he had a reputation as a top player. He was strong and built like a bull. He used to run straight at you. I scored two tries, I stepped him as I certainly didn't want to run straight at him, he would have cut me in two. We lost 30-22.

After a few games on the wing, I was moved inside to centre. The first time I played centre was at home to St Helens. I found out I was going to be up against Australian test centre Michael O'Connor. I said to Foxy: 'Bloody hell Peter, what are you doing here? This man is an international'. I think someone had cried off for Featherstone and as a result I'd been moved inside. Foxy just told me I'd be alright and it turned out I was. I scored a nice try and we ended up winning 13-12. It was intimidating coming through as a kid playing against older, established players. I would sometimes think: 'He's going to kill me here'. My dad used to tell me that it's not as bad as I thought it was going to be. I think it was though. I felt I could handle it, but if somebody clouted me right, I knew about it.

As a young player, I knew there would be an opposition player or two trying to intimidate me. In those days without so much Sky Television coverage and every camera angle imaginable available, players could get away with a sly dig. The older players had their own little tricks. Having said that, apart from cuts and bruises, the only bad injury I had at Featherstone was a dislocated elbow. We were playing Sheffield Eagles at Don Valley. It was a cold night. Don Valley never seemed to be muddy, it always seemed to be a firm, sandy playing surface. I made a break from a scrum up the middle of the park and I thought I was going to score. Keith Mumby came from out of nowhere, dived and tapped my ankles. I fell and all my weight came down onto my arm. My elbow came out. The covering defence jumped on me and I was shouting 'get off my arm'. I was taken to hospital, put to sleep and they put my elbow back in. When I got home, my arm was really swollen. At the time, it was the worst injury I had suffered.

Mind you, I remember getting knocked out by Roy Haggerty. It was at the back end of his career; he was playing for Huddersfield and tackled me. I also remember playing Leeds and I made a break on the stand side of Post Office Road going towards the scoreboard. Carl Gibson tackled me in the corner then Colin Maskill came running across, he just went in and caught me on the back of the head. I woke up in Pontefract Hospital. My mum was there, she never said to me that she was worried I was going to get hurt playing rugby, but she might have said something to my dad.

It was still a winter game then, we would be running in mud and struggled to get going, but somehow we did. I remember an evening game at home to St Helens in December 1990. We were winning easily at half time. It was a really cold night, the frost came out and the Saints lads wouldn't come back on the pitch because they said it was too dangerous to play. We were waiting for them thinking 'we've got these fellows', they eventually came out and ending up giving us a hiding, 33-16. We wished they'd stayed in the dressing rooms.

I was a bit of a goalkicker when I joined Featherstone. Steve Quinn took me for a few goalkicking lessons on the back field at Post Office Road. I kicked nine goals for the club. One day though, against Halifax, I had a kick from the touchline. I was too close to the spectators and they were heckling me and swearing at me. I couldn't concentrate and I missed. After that I told Peter that I didn't want to kick any more. It was too much responsibility. A game can be won or lost on a kick and being so young, I didn't want that on my shoulders. So he took the goalkicking duties away from me. I just used to belt it as hard as I could.

The more I played, the more recognition I would get and the more headlines I would see about myself in the newspapers. People knew who I was and wanted to talk to me about the game. Sometimes, I might even get a pint or two out of it. But it can be a bad thing. I was playing for my local side and in the spotlight all the time. Look at Paul Wellens at St Helens, he lives in the town, does his shopping in the town and goes out round the town. He's got St Helens on him all the time and that's what it was like for me at Featherstone.

At Saints I could play and then come away from St Helens. I could go to the local shop and no-one knew who I was. My dad said to me that when he played for Hull it was great being able to travel back to Pontefract. If he'd had a bad game, he could get away from it. I didn't hear the 'Newlove was useless' comments as I lived away from St Helens.

My name helps me stand out sometimes. The name 'Newlove' is unusual. There are not many Newloves in the telephone book. It can be difficult paying a bill over the phone as women assume the name is 'New' and I am just calling them 'love'. I've also had Truelove printed on letters to me.

It did feel strange when complete strangers would come up to me, I didn't know how they were going to react to me. Some would be nice and friendly but others would say 'who do you think you are?' I just had to walk away from it and sometimes that could be hard. Most of the time, it was alright though and it can help you develop. Some people wanted to talk to me only because I played rugby, but if I got something out of it as well, it's working for both sides. At times, I milked it.

Sometimes though, a lack of recognition could be the problem. I remember one trip to St Helens with Featherstone and I realised in the changing rooms that I had left my shoulder pads on the bus. I nipped out to get them. At the players' entrance at Saints they have commissionaires with fancy army clothes and a sash and all that. When I went back with my pads to try and get in the changing rooms one of these old fellows stopped me. He told me I couldn't come in despite me shouting at him: 'I'm playing'. I was let in eventually.

I played alongside Graham Steadman for one season at Featherstone. He was a great player. I liked him and still do; it was a shame he had to leave the coaching position at Castleford. I know his family well, their Mark used to be one of my best mates. We used to work at a sports centre together. I was on a YTS programme. I just used to walk around the swimming baths and put badminton nets up for £28 a week. I did that for two years. I remember once I was waiting for another bloke to show up by the squash court, I was sat down and ended up falling asleep. The manager's office was overlooking the court and he must have seen me. I'm not the best worker. Again, rugby was my get out clause.

Terry Manning always tells the story about when I was a young lad at the club, aged around 18, and he was an old stager. In those days, we were paid by the club on a Thursday night. He swears blind that once he got my wage packet by mistake. He opened it up and shouted 'bloody hell!' He was going mad that I was on more money than him and I was just starting out in the game. I rang him up asking for my money.

I also played alongside Deryck Fox, who was another big influence on me at Featherstone. You could rely on him, he was a good trainer and a good professional. I also remember playing with Jeff Grayson. He used to take the mickey out of me because I used to run round with him and train with him. He was 40 years old and I was only 18 and I used to say to him: 'This is the right pace for me Jeff'. He used to go mad shouting: 'Bloody hell, get up the front' and I would answer that I wanted to train with him. He gave me a real rollicking once. We had been defending on our own line, the opposition had had two sets of six, and it was the last tackle. I was in the tackle and we got a handover. I didn't get up to play-the-ball properly and the referee penalised us, giving them another set of six. Jeff was furious with me. I was only 18 and felt shocking.

We played in the Yorkshire Cup Final in November 1989. It was my first cup final and the pair of us did a television interview together. It was my first ever interview for a local station. They did it because Jeff was the oldest player in the final and I was the youngest. It was done immediately before we were due to take to the field against Bradford. I must have come across as a right pillock, I didn't have a clue what to say. All the other lads were sat behind the camera watching us. They kept on having to cut and film it again; they used up a lot of tape that day. It wouldn't happen these days, no wonder we lost. We started off the game really well, we were all over them but didn't score a try, and in the end they took the honours. We lost 20-14. But one report said that I "made big strides through the Northern defence" and was one of several Featherstone players who deserved more than a runners-up medal, which was nice. The teams were:

*Featherstone Rovers:* C. Bibb, B. Drummond, I. Ropati, P. Newlove, A. Banks, I. Smales, D. Fox, J. Grayshon, T. Clark, G. Bell, G. Price, G. Booth, P. Smith.
Subs: A. Dakin, A. Fisher.
*Scorers:* Tries: Smith, Ropati. Goals: Fox (3).
*Bradford Northern:* I. Wilkinson, G. Cordle, S. McGowan, R. Simpson, R. Francis, I. Henjak, P. Harkin, K. Skerrett, G. Barraclough, J. Hamer, D. Hobbs, K. Fairbank, J. Pendlebury.
Subs: K. Mumby, P. Medley.
*Scorers:* Tries: Harkin (2), Cordle (2). Goals: Hobbs (2).

Brendan Tuuta was a good player at Featherstone, nicknamed the 'Baby Faced Assassin' due to an incident with Wally Lewis when he played for New Zealand. He was a tremendous servant to the club and well thought of by the supporters. He was incredibly tough and gave his all for the cause. He did get sent off a few times, but that's possible one of the reasons why people loved him at Featherstone, they appreciated a player who was into the physical side of the game.

He got sent off playing Oldham once. He started a big fight and got the red card. Tiny Solomona, the big prop for Oldham, got sent off as well. In those days, they left a crate of ale in the changing rooms for after the game. By the time the game finished Tiny and Tuuts had drunk all this ale and were very happy by the time we got in there.

I'd say the funniest player I knew throughout my career was Gary Rose at Featherstone. He used to come to training and tell all the same jokes over and over again. He would say to you: 'He's got a big head hasn't he?' and you would ask: 'Who?' to get the reply 'Humpty Dumpty'. Then we'd hear him say: 'He's looking for regular nights' and again we'd ask: 'Who?' to hear him say: 'King Arthur'. They were poor jokes, but he made us laugh with them. He sold chicken legs at training, I don't know where he got them from. Players would do things like that back then though to make up their money. They would buy stuff then try to flog it to the rest of the lads at the club.

He even brought his Staffordshire Bull Terrier Bonnie to training with him. It ran onto the field while we were training and Peter Fox went mad, shouting: 'Rosey, get this dog off the field.'

He used to be a boxer before he played rugby and his dad was a boxing trainer. Gary went to fight in America and he always used to tell us about this particular fight. He got knocked out and all he could hear was his dad shouting 'get up at eight'. Gary, on the canvas, answered with 'what time is it now?'

As I was playing part-time at Featherstone, as all the players did then, I had another job during the day. I was a porter at Pontefract hospital for three years. I did an interview with the local press when I was working there and told the guy interviewing me that I'd had to take an amputated leg to the incinerator. It was in a box and it was heavy, I couldn't believe how heavy it was. I didn't know what was in the box at the time, I was shaking it and everything. The bosses read the interview and weren't impressed, they said: 'You can't say this Paul, the family of the person who lost the leg might have been reading'.

I also got in trouble there for cutting up a surgeon in one of those little blue cars they had to use in the hospital grounds. We were only supposed to do five miles an hour in them and I think I was doing 15. I used to get it down this little incline as fast as I could. There was a speed bump at the bottom, it was really high suspension and it would go all over the place. It was only a battery operated car that we used to plug in at night. But if I went down the hill, I could get some speed up.

One of my other jobs was to run with blood supplies between the two sites, the main hospital and the maternity unit. There were supposed to be two porters doing this, but because of cutbacks, it ended up being just me. I had my other duties to do as well so I was on the move all the time. Every Monday morning I was ringing in saying I couldn't come to work due to bumps and bruises from the game the day before.

There was a guy called Martin Ward who, alongside John Joyner, was working in rugby league development. They wanted players to go into the schools and teach league to kids in the Featherstone and Wakefield area. Later we did the same thing at St Helens. I enjoyed doing it, just teaching basic skills to 11-year-olds, it was good for the kids.

Clubs need to do a bit more of that and get a structure in place. They might get kids coming through playing for their school, then local amateur club and on to the local professional side. They should concentrate on local kids instead of going out and signing Australians and Kiwis who half the time are no better than the players we have at home. The RFL should lower the overseas quota so more English lads can have a chance to play. Young English players need the experience and sometimes they can't get it because of an overseas player. Teams want success straight away and it can take a few years to get a young lad to the required standard. Clubs won't wait that long so they recruit overseas.

The Australian club, Wests, came in for me while I was in my first year at Featherstone. That was when I got the reputation of not liking flying. They had made me an offer and I can remember sitting in the plunge bath at Featherstone talking to Peter Fox and I told him that I didn't want to go. I felt I was too young to go there on my own. I was only 18 at the time. Featherstone told Wests that I wasn't coming. However, Wests must have told all their supporters and the press that I was meant to arrive on a particular day, so they must have been confident I was coming.

When I didn't turn up, there was a little snippet in the *Daily Mirror* which said I hadn't come because I was scared of flying. From that day, the story has stuck and I've never been able to shake it off so I've just had to put up with it. If I had a pound for every time someone asks me am I scared of flying I'd be secure financially. The answer is no, I am not scared of flying. I've flown to Australia three or four times, I've been all over the place on holiday.

I had opportunities to play over there since that offer. Do I regret not going? I don't think so; I don't think I've missed anything. The fear of flying myth came up again when I was selected to go to Australia with Great Britain for the World Sevens. I didn't want to go because at the time of the tournament I was moving house. The RFL said it was important. I said: 'Well if it's that important, why isn't Great Britain coach Malcolm Reilly going?' So I didn't go to the Sevens. I got slated for it but at the end of the day, I thought it was a Mickey Mouse competition. I had better things to do than being dragged out there. I had stuff to organise for my move.

It was great getting the Greenalls Young Player of the Year award in 1988-89. I was the youngest-ever winner. Another contender was Gary Connolly. As Gary and I are the same age, we have always been compared to each other and that award probably started it off. We're not enemies, but have always been in opposition with each other, Gary's a good bloke. People always compare us and ask who's better. I thought that Eddie and Stevo always seemed to prefer him to me, but that doesn't really worry me to be honest.

Playing for Yorkshire was a big deal for me. In 1989, I played against Lancashire at Wigan – we won 56-12 and I got two tries. I wish I had been given a cap but they stopped giving them out in favour of handing out a patch for your blazer. My dad has a Yorkshire cap, I've got an England cap and a Great Britain cap and I would have been very proud to have a Yorkshire cap. I was more proud of playing for Yorkshire than I was for Great Britain. Yorkshire used to give Lancashire some real hidings. Foxy was coach of Yorkshire as well, which was good and making that appearance for Yorkshire got me into the Great Britain set up.

Peter Fox left Featherstone to go to Bradford in October 1991, and Alan Agar came in until the end of the season. Unfortunately we were relegated. I never saw Alan smile.

Featherstone were relegated from Division One at the end of the 1991-1992 season. Swinton finished bottom with six points. Above them, four teams had 22 points, but we had the worst points difference so we filled the second relegation spot. Salford, Bradford Northern and Hull were the lucky ones to escape.

I only had a year left on my contract and was happy to see it out, I wanted to come back up with Featherstone and then make my move elsewhere. I was still young, just 21 when the new season started, and wanted to stick it out. I don't think I had any offers to go anywhere else anyway. At the start of the 1992-93 season, Deryck Fox left to go to join Peter Fox at Bradford Northern for a £140,000 transfer fee. He got a bit of stick from the Featherstone fans for jumping ship.

In 1992-93, Featherstone were Division Two champions with Steve Martin as coach. I still hold the tries in a season record at Featherstone with 48 that year. I also scored four in representative matches (three for Great Britain and one for England) which made 52 in total, the joint record for a centre in a season. My winger Owen Simpson got 34 tries in 33 games for Featherstone as well.

We were great that year and had a good side for the Second Division. It wasn't nice playing at some of the grounds that we had to visit for away games.

I remember going to Bramley. There was a car boot sale on the pitch in the morning, after that there was a game of football and then we came on. I don't know how much grass was left on the pitch, but there was dog mess everywhere. The changing rooms were unbelievable, there were some amateur sides with better changing rooms. That's what we were up against at times in the Second Division. Not all the clubs were like that, but many were in those days.

We ended the season at a far better ground: Manchester United's Old Trafford for the Divisional Premiership Final. We got changed at the 'other' Old Trafford, Lancashire County Cricket Club as the football ground dressing rooms were reserved for the First Division teams who played their match after ours.

We beat Workington 20-16. I scored two tries and got the man-of-the-match award. It was a great day. The teams were:

*Featherstone Rovers:* M. Pearson, I. Butt, T. Manning, P. Newlove, O. Simpson, F. Maloney, B. Daunt, L. Casey, M. Wilson, W. Taekata, G. Price, I. Smales, B. Tuuta. Subs: N. Roebuck, R. Gunn.
*Scorers:* Tries: Newlove (2), Maloney. Goals: Pearson (4).
*Workington Town:* M. Mulligan, D. Drummond, T. Kay, B. Hepi, G. Smith, G. Byrne, D. Marwood, J. Pickering, P. McKenzie, P. Riley, I. Scott, C. Armstrong, W. Kitchen.
Subs: G. Schubert, M. Oglanby.
*Scorers:* Tries: McKenzie, Oglanby. Goals: Marwood (4).

After the game, we ran round with the trophy and then it was the First Division Premiership Final between Saints and Wigan. I can remember on my way round, some of the Saints speccies saying 'are you coming to us next season?'

They were about to lose Gary Connolly and I was planning to leave Featherstone. I told them: 'I might be, it's on the cards'. Of course, I ended up at Bradford for a £245,000 transfer fee. Peter Fox got me to Bradford. He was the only reason I signed for them.

I took on an agent when I was leaving Featherstone, but that arrangement didn't work out. The Bradford contract was sorted out by me, my dad and Peter.

I did talk to Mally Kay at St Helens before I signed for Bradford, but they pulled out of the chase to sign me. I could have been at St Helens earlier. I wish I had joined them when I left Featherstone. I would have had a testimonial there as I would have completed 10 years at the club.

When I left Featherstone, Adele, then my girlfriend, now my wife, had her car window put through. We were living in Pontefract and her car was parked in front of our house. We woke up one morning, the window was smashed and there was a house brick on the front seat, but nothing had been taken. It seemed a bit of a coincidence that this happened at the same time that I was leaving Featherstone.

I always used to go for a drink in Pontefract when I played for Featherstone and I did that when I was leaving the club. I was walking by people and all I could hear was 'scab' and 'Judas'. I just thought I'm not having this, I'm going home. I've never been back there for a drink since then. I just don't want to be somewhere where I could get into trouble. It was the same for Graham Steadman when he left the club; he went to Castleford who are Featherstone's most hated rivals so it was probably even worse for him.

It's like the rivalry between Wigan and Saints except there's only three miles between Featherstone and Castleford. The derby matches against Castleford were great. They were generally pretty even, we even had a few draws. I remember one 14-14 draw in March 1989 at Wheldon Road because I scored a try after catching a pass one-handed. The places are so close together and all the hype about the games makes the players more nervous. Living in the area, I knew that everyone supported one team or the other, and everyone I knew was going to be at the game. People I went to school with, my teachers, they were all there. There were sometimes fights breaking out on the terraces. Throughout my career, I always seemed to score against Castleford, no matter who I was playing for. For Featherstone I got eight tries in the four seasons we played against them.

The best try I scored for Featherstone though was against Halifax, I broke through, beat a couple of people and their massive winger Wilf George was chasing me and I didn't want him to catch me so that was spurring me on. It's one of the best tries I've ever scored. Another one that was close to it was when I went the full length of the pitch for Bradford against Castleford in the mud.

Sometimes on the field at Featherstone I felt that the strategy was to take the ball in and give it to Newy. I was young and could run so it wasn't too bad, but later in my career it was a bit hard. People would say 'but you're our main strike weapon' to which I would reply 'that may be, but let's have a game plan please'.

I always said that I don't owe Featherstone anything. I completed my five year contract there and got the club a good transfer fee so I didn't think I had done anything wrong. There were people around the club who criticised me and I don't talk to them now. If someone offered them a better job with more prospects, what would they do? All they could see was blue and white. The same people come over to me these days and I don't give them the time of day. I'll be polite, but there's no chance of an in-depth conversation. It annoyed me because I was there for five years and made friends with people, including the supporters who would come into the bar after the game. It's very rare I go back to Featherstone now, which is a shame because I enjoyed my time there.

Featherstone asked for ridiculous money for me, at one point, I heard that they wanted a million pounds for me. I went to see them and asked where were the wages to reflect what they thought I was worth. I was on about £20,000 a year at most at Featherstone. I thought they were going to price me out of the game.

I actually agreed a contract with Wigan when I was looking to move. I don't know why, but I didn't think they meant it. They were looking around at new players. I think they were hanging on for Gary Connolly rather than trying to sign me.

## Freddie Levine was Featherstone's groundsman for 33 years

*Freddie:* "The first thing I remember about Newy is one of his first games for the club at Halifax. It was a night match and all the players were psyched up, as they would be just before a match. I always thought that Thrum Hall was a tip. Once the players were in the dressing room, I started to put all the gear on the field for the team. All the players were out on the pitch bar one. I thought that with him being a young kid coming into what was a decent team that he would be a bag of nerves. It was a freezing cold night. There was a radiator in the dressing room. I found Newy laid down in front of it fast asleep. How cool is that?"
*Paul:* "Cool? It was freezing."
*Freddie:* "The other thing I can tell you is that he's a tight so-and-so."
*Paul:* "My dad and my uncle Charlie have given me this reputation of 'the Newloves are tight with money' because I think they were the two tightest people in rugby league in those days. I've been tarred with the same brush."
*Freddie:* "You are tight though."
*Paul:* "I'm just careful and cautious."

## John Hill commentates on Featherstone Rovers match videos

*John:* "I first saw Paul play in junior rugby league. Terry Mullaney, who was on the committee at Featherstone, and I saw him play at Normanton. It was a Sunday afternoon and Paul had played tremendously well. I came home, didn't have my dinner and said to Terry that we had to get him signed. We went down to Featherstone to see Peter Fox before the game started that afternoon. I went to the clubhouse and got there before Terry. I saw Peter and said: 'We've just seen this lad play, we've got to sign him on, young Paul Newlove, you coached his dad John'. I then made the fatal mistake of saying: 'he's another Neil Fox'. Peter turned round, very cross, and said: 'there will never, ever be another Neil Fox!' It got my back up a bit and I asked him if he'd seen Paul play. He said he had and I asked 'where?'

Terry later arrived and we saw Richard Evans who was the club chairman. We insisted to Richard that the club had to sign Paul. Richard just said: 'It's up to him' and walked away. In Richard's defence I caught him unawares, he was busy with other things and we were talking about juniors. As luck would have it as we stood at the bar, Bob Ashby, the Featherstone president came in. Terry told Bob about Paul and Bob went to sign him. If it hadn't have been for Bob we wouldn't have signed Paul."

*Paul:* "That's true and it was Bob's own money he used for the signing on cheque."

*John:* "The try he scored against Halifax as a young kid is one of the best tries I've ever seen. I've been a supporter of the game for 50 years. Paul didn't only score tries though; he made a load of tries for his wing partner at Fev, Owen Simpson. Paul was powerful and deceptively quick for a big man. Every time he touched the ball something could happen. He was one of those players who you could keep quiet for 79 minutes, but in the last minute he'd win the match. He's a legend in the game and one of the best players that Featherstone Rovers have ever produced. I remember Paul playing for Fev against Hull. It was really foggy and the game should have been called off. I was commentating and Hull kicked the ball into touch. I said: 'It'll be Deryck Fox to feed the scrum' and the timekeeper, who was sitting next to me, asked in amazement 'can you see Deryck Fox from here?' I replied 'no but I know he feeds the scrums.'

We were playing at Bramley and Paul needed one try to break the record for tries in a season at the club. Brett Daunt, our Australian scrum half, broke through and he was under the sticks. He waited there so he could give Paul the ball for the try he needed."

*Paul:* "I chased Brett shouting: 'Don't put it down! Don't put it down!'"

*John:* "For an Aussie to do that for an Englishman is unusual."

*Paul:* "I beat Shaun Edwards for top-try-scorer that year." [Paul won the Stones Bitter top try scorer award. At £30 per try, this was worth £1,560].

*John:* "Later in his career, I watched Paul play for St Helens in Challenge Cup Finals and I really hoped he would get a try at Wembley. His dad scored three tries at Wembley, two in 1973 and one in 1974, but Paul never got one there."

*Paul:* "I would have loved to have scored in a Wembley Challenge Cup Final or in a Grand Final, but it never happened."

# 3. Birth of the Bulls

When I had signed my five-year deal with Featherstone, my dad said: 'If you haven't made it by the time you're 21, you're probably not going to make it.' Backs seem to make their mark in the game at a younger age than forwards. When the five years were up, it was time to leave. I had to move on to better myself. I signed for Bradford on 13 July 1993 and I remember people saying: 'What have you gone there for? They're no better than Featherstone'. The transfer fee, which was agreed by a RFL Tribunal, was £245,000.

That first season though, Bradford finished joint top of the league with Warrington and Wigan, with Wigan claiming the title on points difference alone. It haunts me to this day. I still think about it because we played bottom-of-the-league Leigh at Odsal that season and lost 14-24. They only won one other league game all season. We beat all the top sides and we lost to Leigh. Wigan were full-time and had proper weights programmes, so to get that close to them was unbelievable. Wigan always had the luck as well I thought. If they were losing they always seemed to clinch it in the end. They always kept their composure, which is the sign of a good side. They had a side full of internationals, how could we compete with that?

1994 Stones Bitter Championship

|  | Played | Points | For | Against | Difference |
|---|---|---|---|---|---|
| 1. Wigan | 30 | 46 | 780 | 403 | 377 |
| 2. Bradford Northern | 30 | 46 | 784 | 555 | 229 |
| 3. Warrington | 30 | 46 | 628 | 430 | 198 |

I would have liked to have won a trophy at Bradford with Peter. I enjoyed my time there. It was a bigger club with better facilities than Featherstone. I used to hang round with Deryck Fox, Karl Fairbank, Jon Hamer and Roy Powell. Our wives and kids all got on with each other. We used to sit together in the family bit after the game, the rest of the players were single lads and Australians. David Hobbs was there. He's from Featherstone and for the first few training sessions I went to his house for him to take me to training until I learnt how to get there.

Karl Fairbank was a tremendous professional and real workhorse in the forwards, as well as scoring some tries for the club. He is a farmer and has big, farming hands. I enjoyed playing with him for Great Britain too. Big Roy Powell, God bless him, was a gentleman. One unusual thing about him was that he was always last out of the changing rooms, even on training nights.

I remember we used to play hell with the conditioner at Featherstone because we thought his sessions were boring. We usually knew what we were going to do before we turned up at training. Of course, he moved to Bradford with Peter Fox. So when people ask if training was different at Bradford, I can say no, it definitely wasn't. It only changed when the clubs were gearing up for Super League and Matthew Elliott came to Bradford to put in the groundwork for the arrival of new coach Brian Smith. When that happened, the club went full-time. We used to train in the morning; then have an hour or two break before coming back in the afternoon. Often a few of us went to the snooker hall on Odsal Top for a couple of hours, then come back to the club for the afternoon's work.

Foxy had sorted my contract out and he told me that I needed a job. To top my contract up, they got me a job with Graham Jennings' roofing firm. Jenno was on the Bradford board at the time. He had a depot at Leeds so I had to go there. The first day I went with the driver to Manchester. We had to unload two thousand roof tiles. We went to this building site and get them off the lorry and passing the slates through a chain of us on to the roofers on the scaffolding. It was hard work. I came home and the next day I ended up in the yard driving a fork lift truck trying to move the roof tiles stacked on pallets. I smashed more than I moved. I'd never driven one before and no one was there to supervise me. With there being no one there I kept on nipping home, I would start late and finish early. After three days, Jenno told me: 'It's not working out this' and that was it, I never went back. Foxy never said anything, just tutted and shook his head.

My Bradford debut was against Widnes at Odsal on 29 August 1993. We won 32-18 and I scored a try. I was trying so hard to score and impress, but nothing went right for me. It was the back end of the second half when I finally stumbled over. It wasn't a good try, but I was off the mark for my new club.

The first time I went back to Featherstone with Bradford I couldn't play as the Rugby Football League had banned me for the weekend because I had refused to play for Great Britain in the World Sevens in Australia. I asked to run on with the sand for

Bradford and rub it in a bit. It was the first time I've ever done anything like that because it can come back to haunt you. I didn't really think about the consequences. It was cold, but I took my coat off and kept my Bradford tracksuit on. When I made my playing return there the next season, my opposite number Andy Currier got sent off for a head high tackle on me.

Odsal could be hard to play on when it was cold but the coldest ground I ever played on was Thrum Hall against Halifax on Boxing Day 1994. There was snow, sleet, everything. It felt like the coldest place on earth. I scored two tries and we drew the game. The first try I scored was a good one. I took John Bentley on, pushed him off and went half the length of the field. It was good because running for it probably stopped me from being frozen into a block of ice like Captain Caveman.

Odsal was weird when it was foggy, all round the top would be clear but when you looked into the bowl it would be filled with fog. We were playing Wigan one night and the game got called off after 10 minutes due to fog. We were winning as well when it got called off. It was pretty thick though.

I was there at the birth of the Bulls as the club changed its name and image from Bradford Northern as part of the introduction of Super League in 1996. It had a great impact and added to the atmosphere. Bradford have tremendous crowds today because of what the club did then. They have a lot of space in Odsal and use it well with gimmicks. I think they've done a good job. Sometimes in the early days they would give tickets away to get people into some games and make the ground look full. But they don't need to do that now. All the Super League clubs are into the razzmatazz now. Most supporters love it, that's what they pay their money for. They watch top quality rugby league and enjoy all the entertainment for the kids too, it's a complete night out. The day may come when we see some spectacular trapeze artist in St Helens. They've had skydivers in the past, how spectacular is that?

The birth of the Bulls also meant that the players received new clothing and training gear which was a great improvement. All we had to do was turn up for training and everything was on our pegs ready for us. Everything was washed for us after training. I also had a sponsored Mercedes at Bradford. It was a lovely car. I used to play on the golf days with the sponsors; they told me that they used to sponsor Will Carling. We certainly didn't have that at Featherstone.

One of the players I played with at Bradford was Dave Watson who had unreal talent. Watto was one of those players who didn't need to train. He could just literally turn up and play. He worked well with me. He would run across the pitch and give me little drop-off balls and that's how I scored a few of my tries at the club. He played really well for Bradford and the supporters loved him there. He was bit of a wildcard as well, he liked to go out.

When Robbie Paul came to the club, he was only around 17-years-old. Peter Fox didn't put him in the team straight away, which I thought was right because he was only small then, he still had a lot of growing to do. He was quick and I could see he was going to make it. Peter was trying to hold him back and look after him. I believe Peter took some criticism over this as a lot of people wanted Robbie in the side. Robbie has ended up as a long-term servant to the club. He's one of the few players today who has stayed at one club for a long time and that's a credit to him.

I played alongside Neil Holding at Bradford. He scored a try in the last game of our 1993-94 league campaign – a 52-10 triumph at Leeds. He always used to have his socks rolled down. He would run about as if he was hunched up. Much earlier in my career, I had played against him when I was at Featherstone and he was at St Helens. He had been on the bench for them and we were winning. They put him on and he changed the game, created lots of opportunities for Saints and they won. He was a good player and a real joker. He did impressions and was a good person to have in our dressing room. At Bradford, he was assistant coach to Nigel Stephenson with the 'A' team. We must have had injuries in the side for Neil to come in at that stage of his career.

Brian McDermott was another character. He was usually good to get on with. He used to be a boxer. He was always joking, messing about and taking the mickey out of himself and other players. He is a good lad.

One of my wing partners at Bradford was Brimah Kebbie. He was well-to-do from 'down south' and very intelligent. He had a lot of pace and scored a few tries. However, he nearly lost me as his centre as Peter Fox tried me at stand off for a while. He had previously tried this move at Featherstone. I told him I didn't think it was working and he said that was what my dad had said when Peter had moved him to stand off, yet he went on to do well in the position. I was a different sort of player though, which Peter realised and he put me back to centre.

Trevor Clark, the Kiwi hooker at Bradford, was out with me one night. I wasn't drinking but he was. I ended up driving him home in the early hours. The police pulled me over, they saw us in our suits and with me driving my Mercedes they must have thought I looked like a pimp. The police saw some empty beer bottles in the back of the car, but realised I hadn't been drinking and let us get on our way.

I once got chucked out of a Leeds nightclub because of who I was. I asked why I was being chucked out and he said 'because you're Paul Newlove' and I asked what was wrong with that. He told me that people would try and pick fights with me, so they wanted me to go. We gave him the slip and dodged the bouncer all night as he tried to come and look for me. In the end, I left of my own accord as I got fed up of running away from him.

While at Bradford, we had a fun weekend at Ampleforth. It was probably just to keep us out of mischief. Foxy took us there and set up various activities. We went to the gym and did circuit training. Peter always liked to have relay races after training to keep the squad's morale up. It was very entertaining. I was one of the passengers in a group that decided to 'borrow' one of the younger squad member's cars on the Saturday night. Around Ampleforth, there was a little village pub, but rugby league players in their early twenties want a bit more nightlife so we took the car to York. We came back later that night in the car to discover that the player in question was visibly upset over the disappearance of his vehicle. The next morning the bus was ready to take us back to Bradford. Carl Hall and I were still asleep in our room. I can remember Foxy's booming, Yorkshire voice shouting: 'Get up, get up!' We hadn't packed, so it was a rush job to get onto the bus.

While I was at Bradford, Carl Winterburn and I bought some cows. Carl signed for Bradford just after I did. I didn't know him before that, we became mates though. I still knock about with him now. Carl had bought a smallholding of around 20 acres and we thought we'd buy some cows and keep them there. With having Karl Fairbank and Paul Dixon at the club who were both farmers, we thought we would be alright. We had about 25 cows, which we thought was the most we could have on the land we had. It was a hobby I enjoyed.

Bradford against Leeds games were big occasions. As with Featherstone and Castleford, or Saints and Wigan, the two cities aren't far apart, there was always a full house. Bradford played

Leeds at Bradford City FC's Valley Parade in November 1993. The ground was packed and we beat Leeds 36-28 that day, Roy Powell scored in the closing moments of the game. He stretched out his big arm and plonked the ball down. They were hard games but there again, all derbies are. The players get more stick from the away supporters too in a derby. The Bradford fans were solid, they always got behind the side.

Peter Fox ended up having trouble at Bradford after the club extended his contract. Peter came to me and said he had extended his contract, would I do the same? I told him no worries, Foxy sorted me out with a contract. A week or two later, they sacked Foxy. We thought that they had only extended Peter's contract to get me to sign. A bit later, Peter asked me if I wanted to leave Bradford because he had been talking about me to people at St Helens. I just wanted to get away from Bradford, it wasn't the same for me after Peter left.

Mal Kay played a big part in me coming to St Helens, he was pushing for me all the time as did Tom Ellard. Tom came to the contract meetings with Mal Kay. He helped sell the club to me. During the World Cup I had been in Chris Joynt and Bobbie Goulding's room asking what Saints was like. I think Bobbie knew I was on the verge of signing, so maybe he paid me a bit more attention to get me on board. Maybe Mal Kay had told him to be nice to me.

In the end, in November 1995, I got away from Bradford and Paul Loughlin, Sonny Nickle and Bernard Dwyer left Saints and went the other way. I think that kick started Bradford to get them where they are today. Those three players made the club stronger, plus they got all that money as well. I reckon I did them a good turn. The £500,000 deal is still the world record to this day and with big transfer fees seemingly a thing of the past, it will probably not be beaten. Saints paid £250,000 – Paul, Sonny and Bernard made up the rest of the fee.

Brian Smith phoned me at home before I left the club, I can't remember the details, but he was giving me a right rollicking. I couldn't really commit to Brian because I was so far down the track towards joining St Helens. I dealt with Matthew Elliott who had come along to set things up for Brian's arrival. I thought I got on with Matthew. So Brian Smith didn't really get the best out of me as I had decided I wanted to leave. I got 66 tries in 67 starts for Bradford which isn't too bad.

**Adele Newlove has known Paul since they were 15 and they got married in 2002. They have two children, Chloe and Joe.**

*Adele:* "It can be hard going to matches sometimes. When we went back to Featherstone with Bradford, some supporters knew who we were and were abusive. It's not great, particularly when I had our children with me.

It can be interesting when supporters don't know who I am. Paul was playing for St Helens against Castleford and I was sitting in the stand. This lad started telling me he was Paul's best mate and that Paul wouldn't be staying at Saints for much longer, as he couldn't stand the travelling. I was just going 'Oh yeah, really'. It's interesting when you stand among the supporters and they don't know who you are because you hear what they're saying."

*Paul:* "I wouldn't know. I'm in the safest place, on the pitch."

*Adele:* "We had some good laughs at Featherstone. It was interesting going from Featherstone to Bradford to St Helens; three very different clubs. When we went to Old Trafford with Featherstone, we noticed the difference in the clubs' calibre. Featherstone came down as if we were on a pub day out and in the club after, we saw all the Wigan and Saints players, these two big clubs, it was a bit intimidating. At Featherstone, everybody knew each other and we could just walk into the club. All of a sudden at Bradford, doormen were asking us for passes. It was good that Deryck Fox was already there when Paul signed, as I knew his wife Alison. Featherstone was so close to us that Bradford seemed like a fair way away, yet it was only about half an hour. It's funny looking back because we then had eight years travelling to and from St Helens.

Peter Fox has been brilliant to us. He's gone with Paul when he had to go in front of the disciplinary committee, put him in touch with a financial advisor and told him to get a pension. Whatever comes up, we would just say 'let's ask Peter'. He's wonderful.

People can't believe that Paul doesn't watch games at home. But if he worked in a doughnut factory, he wouldn't come home and make them all night would he? Once he's come home, he's not bothered. Rugby league supporters can't understand it. But when he was playing, he was focussed. In the build-up to a game, Paul would never go anywhere, he wouldn't speak, he wouldn't do anything at all."

**Peter Fox was Paul's coach for Featherstone Rovers, Bradford Northern and Yorkshire.**

*Peter:* I first saw Paul play for the juniors in Featherstone and there were three lads that were signed by the club. Paul was the only one I really wanted. I knew he would make it. I spoke to Paul's dad to see if Paul would join us, his dad said that he would like Paul to be coached by me.

I heard that Hull had offered Paul more money than we had. The club agreed to offer him a better contract and he signed. He played in the 'A' team for a couple of games, and then I put him into the first team. One of his first games was on the wing against then Great Britain winger Des Drummond when we played Warrington. Paul left him for dead and scored two tries. Paul showed his pace and strength and never looked back. I knew he had the ability to go all the way.

Paul was a devastating finisher who could finish from a long way out. He scored a lot of great tries for us. One that sticks out for me was away at London for Bradford in the Regal Trophy in 1993. The pitch was heavy going and we were losing. Paul scored a tremendous try from 75 yards out. I have no end of memories of Paul like that. He was no problem at all to coach; he did everything you required of him. He's had a great career. Paul played alongside Deryck Fox and Fox was the first man who would look to the right and kick to the left for Paul to chase the kick and score."

*Paul:* "Andrew Johns and everyone else do it now, but we did it years ago. It was a planned move: the reverse kick."

*Peter:* "We were the first to use it. Mind you, if there had been the number of cameras there are today, they might have found Paul offside once or twice."

*Paul:* "After training sessions, we used to have relay races in competition with the 'A' team coach and Foxy used to pick the teams. He would always pick all the fast players for his team. He would pick me, Owen Simpson, all the best runners and say 'let's have a fiver on this'."

*Peter:* "Later, when I was coach at Bradford, I was at Wembley doing some work for the BBC and I spoke to Eric Ashton, who took me over to the St Helens board and I spent half an hour convincing them that they should sign Paul, who was coming to the end of his contract at Featherstone.

They were about to lose Gary Connolly to Wigan, so they were going to have some money to spend. I went back to the Bradford board and said St Helens are going to sign Paul Newlove and why should I as Bradford coach help them get the best centre there's going to be in the game for the next few years? I said 'why don't we sign him?'"

*Paul:* "Can you remember in 1994 we were top of the league with Wigan, but they won the title on points' difference? We beat Wigan that year, we beat Leeds, can you remember who we lost to?"

*Peter:* "Leigh!"

*Paul:* "Leigh at home and Hull away, they were the two bottom sides, if it wasn't for those two Foxy..."

*Peter:* "I know, I know."

*Paul:* "That's one of my biggest disappointments in rugby."

*Peter:* "You have to overcome these things though, it wasn't a level playing field, Wigan had all the money and were full-time. I had no money to spend at Bradford.

When I was leaving Bradford, I thought that I didn't want to leave my main asset there when I had brought him to the club. I rang Eric Hughes, the Saints coach at the time. I told him that two years back, they had wanted to buy Paul Newlove and would have paid around £250,000 for him. Now they would pay the same amount and offload three players which would make the deal worth half a million pounds. He told me it was a lot of money but I explained in terms of cash, they would still only be paying £250,000. He said 'what about the three players we're letting go?' I said 'if you're prepared to let them go, they're worth nothing to you, so you're still only paying £250,000'. They did the deal.

I always just tried to look after Paul's career and guide him along the right lines. I told him he mustn't retire, until he had to because he would be a long time retired.

We took him to Castleford for his last year, closer to home and a chance to give a helping hand to a club that needed it. He could have gone to Hull a month later, but we had agreed he would go to Castleford."

*Paul:* "Now my playing career has finished, do you think I could be a coach, Peter?"

*Peter:* "No. You could coach kids though. You've always been a players' player that people have been pleased to have at their club."

### Carl Hall was one of Paul's team mates at Bradford

*Carl:* "I first met Paul when I signed for Bradford in 1994. We went to training together because we lived close to each other. We got on well, later on we had St John Ellis travelling with us for a couple of months and he did our heads in."

*Paul:* "He never stopped talking."

*Carl:* "Paul was quiet until he had a few drinks. I don't think people realised how good a player he was. We did as we played with him week in, week out. He was unbelievable sometimes. He didn't always do much in some games, but what he did was spectacular. We played Castleford on a muddy surface and he went the length of the field for a great try. He was very, very lazy in training though. Going to St Helens was the best thing for him as he became fitter and stronger. Before we used to go to training at Bradford, we used to stop at the chip shop and get fish butties."

*Paul:* "I remember one session where we had some food from the chippy before training, thinking we would be alright. The session turned out to be a tough one and I was nearly retching with this food inside me. We used to go for a fry up in a café at Odsal Top on a Saturday morning. They were alright with us in there and had a bit of banter with us. Some lads would order the full breakfast, we never used to think about our diet in those days. I nearly said the old days but that makes me sound like I'm 102 years old."

*Carl:* "Our birthday is on the same day although I'm younger than him."

*Paul:* "Rubbish." [Carl is older than Paul.]

*Carl:* "We left Bradford within two weeks of each other. Brian Smith was giving us both a bit of a hard time. I don't know whether we were a bit too laidback for him. We went to training one day and Paul told Brian he would be right for the Sheffield game. Brian said 'you'll be right if I pick you'. Paul was a bit cross about this, I think that was the final straw. I scored a try in that game and Paul scored three. That was one of his last games for Bradford. He went to St Helens and I joined Leeds.

I remember Brian Smith being put in his place by the Bradford groundsman Freddie. The groundsman turned up late one morning to open up. Smithy tried to give him a rollicking, but Freddie simply said: 'I'll open the doors when I want to open the doors'. He's still at the club now and is fantastic.

I went to St Helens with Paul when he signed for them. We came back to a pub near my place and had a few drinks and played pool. On the television news in the pub were shots of Paul climbing out of a security van at St Helens, which gave me a laugh. Kevin Iro, who is another friend of mine, kept hounding me when I joined Leeds to get Paul to come to the club because he wanted to play alongside him. He organised a meeting with Dean Bell which I tried to get Paul to come to, but he didn't as he was contracted to St Helens. The pair ended up playing together at St Helens and were brilliant, so it all worked out well in the end.

Paul and Kevin came to stay with me in Paris in 1999 after their Grand Final win over Bradford. I was playing union for Stade Francais at the time. We went out on a big drinking session around Champs Élysées, starting around midday. Paul was walking round with a huge cigar that must have cost about £50. We ended up in a Karaoke bar and Paul slurred to me and Kevin that he had a good song. He then performed the Elvis classic *(Marie's the name) His Latest Flame* while also trying - and failing - not to fall over. After this, he disappeared. Kevin and I went to look for him. He wasn't back at the car or the Karaoke bar, Kevin started to get annoyed at me for losing Paul.

We have no idea how Paul had worked out where I lived or how he had got past the alarm system on the outside of the building, but we could tell he was there. This was because we followed the distinct trail up the stairs that Paul had left. At the top was Paul, passed out. He had got a taxi home and when the taxi driver asked him for 80 francs, Paul paid £80. The next morning, suffering with a bad hangover, Paul insisted that the taxi driver had robbed him. I drove him and Kevin to the airport and Paul had his head out of the window being sick as a dog for most of the trip. Paris is traffic mad, so you can imagine the reaction. He was white as a ghost."
*Paul:* "On the flight home, I never moved. The bloke sitting next to me thought I must be travel sick and I just went along with it. The shots we had at the Karaoke bar tasted like pop. It was only when I tried to walk away that I realised that I no longer had legs.

Top: My dad John – when playing for Featherstone Rovers
Bottom left: My uncle Charlie Stone at Hull
Bottom right: Peter Fox (left) with Jimmy Thompson and the
Championship Trophy at Bradford Northern
(Photos: Courtesy Robert Gate)

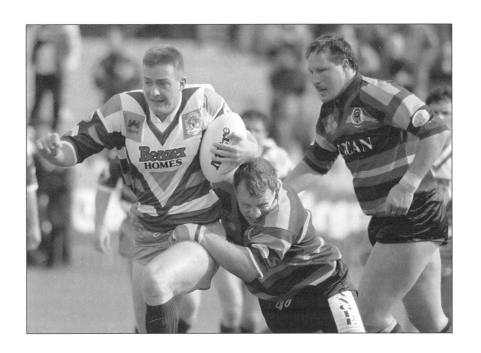

Going forward for Featherstone
(Photos: David Williams)

Playing for Bradford Northern at Odsal
(Photo: David Williams)

# 4. Around the world

I made a record eight appearances for the Great Britain under-21 side. I think I was stuck in there too long. I made my debut in my first season at Featherstone, and played my last game in 1992. I did enjoy it, although I used to hate playing in France. Nice country, nice place to go on holiday, but to play rugby there is not nice. They were often a dirty side. In my second match, in February 1989 in Carpentras, there was a big brawl which started in our own 25. We had Timmy Street in our team who was certainly handy in those situations. Everyone was involved in this fight with the French running in and kicking us then running off. We carried on fighting until we pushed them back to the half-way line. It took ages to split the sides up. The French would poke you in the eye, pull your hair, they were really bad on their own soil. The other thing is, I believe that some of their players were over the age limit. It didn't make a difference though, as we usually beat them.

The food wasn't brilliant. They couldn't even get beans on toast right. All we lived on was crusty bread and orange juice, not the ideal way to go into a game. It's just not the same as playing in your own country.

On 21 October 1989 I became the youngest Great Britain international at 18 years and 72 days old, when I played against New Zealand at Old Trafford. I was pleased by this as it is a great honour to represent your country. I also received a bonus that was in my contract at Featherstone if I ever played for Great Britain. I was nervous, but not overawed. I was a substitute that day and was sitting on the bench with only minutes left, dying to get on the field. There was only four minutes left and Malcolm Reilly put me on. I nearly scored. Someone put a kick through, I chased it and the Kiwi full back Tony Kemp just got across to shield the ball before I could get a hand to it. I didn't have enough time on the field to make an impression. I made my full debut a week later.

Going into the Great Britain dressing room beforehand was hard. I was a bit shy, maybe that was one of my downfalls. I was suddenly mixing with all the top Wigan players as they made up a large part of the British side at that time, players such as Martin Offiah and Shaun Edwards were there. I felt as if I shouldn't be there, I was just a normal kid from Pontefract playing for a miners' village side. I had to grit my teeth and get through it. Garry Schofield was always alright with me, he talked to me. The Yorkshire lads made me feel welcome. I felt there were cliques in the international set up, and that some of the Wigan players were a clique. I didn't feel comfortable and that's why I didn't go on the New Zealand tour in 1990.

I pulled out after being selected. Malcolm Reilly rang me up to tell me I was making a big mistake by not going. I told him that they say people learn from their mistakes. I thought that maybe he wouldn't pick me again after that.

Generally, Malcolm was fine with me. He tried to get me to sign for Newcastle Knights when he was over there coaching. He came to our house with his wife when he knew he had the Newcastle job. He had information on Newcastle and a video about the place. It showed the beach and everything. I told him it looked great, but I wouldn't be going. It just wasn't for me.

I scored a hat trick for Great Britain against France at Leeds in 1993 when we won 72-6. That stands out in my international career. I won the British Coal man-of-the-match award that day and was given a big old-fashioned miner's lamp from sponsors British Coal. Ellery was selected for the team, but there were problems before the game. Malcolm Reilly had told us not to leave the hotel and Ellery went home as he only lived up the road. Ellery didn't play as a result, so I never played with him. It's a shame as it would been a great experience. When I made my appearance for Yorkshire against Lancashire at Central Park, he was injured.

To be truthful, I felt that the 1992 tour was going to be a long period away from home. I had to go; I had no way of getting out of it. I remember the day we set off from Central Park. All the players' wives were there waving us off, the bus was loaded up then pulled away. I thought: 'Right, this is it, three months'.

Before I left for the tour I was round at my mate Chris Todd's house and I asked what could I do as a sign to him when on television overseas. He said I should put my thumb to my nose and waggle my fingers at the camera. I said: 'Oh yeah, no problem' laughing and joking with him. I told him I would think of something while I was over there and that he should watch out for it. When the test match came round, we were lined up for the national anthem and as the camera panned down the line, I realised I had nothing else planned, so I did the gesture Chris had suggested. If people watch the tapes they will see it. My mates were all laughing back home. It became a sort of trademark. I tried to make it a bit more subtle by doing it while wiping the top of my nose. Tour manager Maurice Lindsay cottoned on and sent a message onto the field before one game telling me not to do it, so I gave it a miss that day.

We had 12 days in Papua New Guinea which was really boring. We couldn't go out of the hotel at night because it was dangerous. The only place we could go was a yacht club; even then we were driven there in minibuses. There was nothing to do there, after training we just lay about in the hotel. The heat and humidity were unbelievable.

We drove in from the airport on a dusty road with jungle on either side with huts and shacks dotted about; it's a third world country. They had stalls where they would sell little birds; I don't know whether they were for eating. I found it a complete culture shock. They love their rugby league over there though. One day, we went for a walk and all the locals were going mad trying to meet us.

Papua New Guineans, generally, are small and when they saw this six foot odd tall black man - Roy Powell - they were ecstatic. They loved him.

The locals used to chew betel nut. It's like a drug to them. They chewed it for awhile, then spit it out. All over the place on the streets we would see these big red tobacco-like things. It stains their teeth red as well.

The crowds for our games over there were very enthusiastic, the grounds were packed. If they would not get into the grounds, they climbed up the trees to get a good view. There would be 20 of them in one tree and if the ball got kicked in there, they would all have to jump down. We played up in the mountains, using little aeroplanes to get there. Each plane only held 14 players, so just the team went, not the full touring squad. After the game, all the locals ran on to the pitch because there were no barriers. Sonny Nickle got hammered with them all overenthusiastically patting him on the back. They thought they were being friendly, but I am not too sure Sonny liked it. We just had to run off the pitch as quickly as we could. There were no changing rooms, so we got changed at the hotel.

One story that sticks out during my time there involved the training gear and training boots we get on tour. One player threw a boot to the speccies, they were fighting over it. This kid won. The player said to the kid: 'Do you want the other one?' while hanging it out of the bus window. The little fellow ran down the street following the bus to try and get the boot. The bus slowed down, letting him catch up then just before he could get hold of the boot, we would speed away again. The poor sod ran all the way back to the hotel and the player gave him the boot saying 'you deserve it old lad'. He had never given up.

I roomed with Daryl Powell on tour. I get on with Daryl, he comes from the same area as me. He was playing for Sheffield Eagles, not one of the bigger clubs, so was from the same background as me. He is a bit older than me and helped me through the tour with things like washing my training gear and so on. But I don't think I ironed anything during the whole tour.

There were times when I found the tour really dragging. I made a calendar to count the days off. I'm sure there were other players who were doing the same.

The big game of the tour was the second test in Melbourne. We had lost the first 22-6, so were desperate for a win. We beat Australia 33-10 in front of thousands of travelling British fans on a wet night. It was an Aussie Rules ground, so the playing area was round, which was a new experience for us. There was a square in the middle of the pitch which was rock hard from where the umpire in Aussie Rules bounces the ball. That win was amazing. We really gave it to them. I scored and although Garry Schofield tried to claim it, it was my try. Shaun Edwards kicked through and we both went for the ball, I got downward pressure on it. I'm having that one. Garry scored our next one anyway. I still have a picture of the changing room afterwards where a crate of beer had been opened and me, Gary Connolly, Kelvin Skerrett and Daryl Powell were starting on the beer and celebrating.

The media attention rugby league receives in Australia is amazing compared to here. Journalists would sometimes twist words to get a story out of something or drop us in it. I did a couple of interviews in Australia because I was one of the youngest players. To be fair they just asked about which clubs were interested in signing me which wasn't too bad.

The third test was at Lang Park in Brisbane, a game which, sadly, we lost 16-10. Bradley Clyde was in his prime then and was a tremendous player. Meninga was my opposite centre and he was amazing to play against. Later in my career, I started hearing the words that I was the 'new Meninga'. I've always ignored stuff like that. It's a lovely comment to hear, but I was nothing like him. I wasn't half as big as him... but I'll accept the comment. He was intimidating to play against, just huge. I didn't make many breaks past him. Australia have so much strength in depth. Their team are all quality players.

I played in the first test in New Zealand and was dropped for the second. I had to play in the midweek team who flew up to Christchurch. We played up there, won and flew back. The second test was the last game of the tour, so training for the midweek side finished. We had played our last game so I decided to go out for a drink. I went out with Graham Hallas and had a good time. Then someone pulled out of the test team and I was in. I said 'No chance'. I sat on the bench and thankfully, only came on for the last nine minutes. We won and I got winning pay for a few minutes work. Someone could have warned me beforehand that I should not to go out as I had a chance of being called up because someone was feeling a bit dodgy.

I was relieved to go home after the tour. It was hard work while we were out there. We would get up early for training and could train three times a day. It was tiring, but it was a wonderful experience. Through rugby league I've seen parts of the world that I wouldn't have done without the game, such as Papua New Guinea. Then there were Australia and New Zealand, which other people have to pay to go to and we got it all for nothing. It was a long way to go and we were representing our country, so I'm definitely glad I did it.

I'm in the British Lions Association which Ray French runs. We meet up before international games and are put up in a hotel. The past Lions have a reunion. They also hold dinners and golf days.

In 1994 the first test against Australia was held at Wembley and we went down to London to do a promotion for the game with Cliff Richard who was going to be singing at the game. I was there along with Phil Clarke, Jonathan Davies and our coach Ellery Hanley. The RFL had a double decker bus outside Wembley and the photographers were taking pictures of Cliff on the bus. The journalists were saying: 'Come on Cliff, sing *Summer Holiday*' and he replied: 'I haven't sung it for that many years that I don't know the words'. I suppose that he has so many songs it is hard to remember, like me trying to remember about all the games I've played in. So in that way Cliff and I have got something in common! He didn't know what rugby league was though. I was half expecting him to come over and say 'Good luck with the horses, I hope you win by four frames to two'. There was a big crowd on the day of the Test, which we won 8-4. I missed that game, but played in the next two, when we were well beaten.

In 1995 Diana Ross was invited to the opening game of the World Cup, England versus Australia at Wembley. She was singing in the back of a vintage car as the two teams walked out around her. She was all done up, but looked a bit thin to me. I'm sure I saw her double once in the St Helens nightclub Crystals.

In the game, I made an interception and my try proved the decisive score for England to win 20-16. When I took the ball I still had some work to do. I had made the ball interception just off centre from the middle of the park, Jim Dymock passed it and I took the ball. I ran in an Ellery Hanley like sideways motion to end up in the far left hand corner. It wasn't a straightforward try. Scoring at Wembley was a tremendous feeling. The try became part of BBC Television's *Grandstand* opening credits for a few weeks. Every time it came on I would say: 'Watch, watch, I'm here'. When I scored there was a camera right in front of me as I dived in. I got in the World XIII selected by a panel of journalists and coaches. That was a great achievement. Phil Larder was England coach and he didn't really inspire me. He was there and I would listen and look like I was interested. I got the opening try of the semi-final against Wales at Old Trafford. Wales were a good side and it was a tough game. We won 25-10 to reach the final. I don't know what odds I was to score the first try, but some of my mates won some money backing me.

The tournament was a good one to play in, but as a World Cup there was only really four or five nations that could field a quality side and at times the rest were just making up the numbers. We played Fiji at Central Park, and won 46-0. They could knock us about, but their rugby ability wasn't really up to scratch.

A topless streaker ran on during the World Cup Final. It was reported later that she was Australian; it was hard to tell at the time as she didn't have any colours on. I wanted to have a double take and look again but I couldn't as there was a scrum and I needed to concentrate. She went the full length of the field, she was a good 'un. I scored a try early in the second half in the bottom left hand corner of the ground. We were tackled just short of the line and I decided to have a go myself. It was a bit risky as if I had been tackled I would have been put into touch, there wasn't much room down the blind side. I don't think they expected me to do it but I had the strength and power to knock Brett Dallas out of the way to score. We fancied ourselves for winning the World Cup as not all their stars played due to the ARL / Super League war down under. Having said that, I wouldn't call them a weakened side, they still had a good team. Beating them in the first game increased our confidence too, but they won the final 16-8. My try had made the score 10-8, but they clinched the game with 13 minutes left.

I played for England in the mid season 1996 European Championship. It was badly timed as it clashed with the Euro 96 football tournament that gripped the country. We played France at Gateshead, and won 73-6. It wasn't a contest. Their team was poor. Emlyn Hughes was there and was a guest in the Sky studio. He said the French were tackling like 'women'. He was sitting on the touchline side watching the game. I scored two tries, but it wasn't a game that stands out for me.

I pulled out of the 1996 Kiwi tour with a hamstring injury. That was the tour where the RFL sent players home near the end to save money. It seemed a bit of a farce. That must have been the worst tour ever so I don't think I missed anything.

Then came the 1997 Australian Super League touring side who we played in three Tests. Andy Goodway was in charge of the Great Britain side. We won the second Test at Old Trafford 20-12, but lost the first 38-14 and the third 37-20. For the first Test at Wembley, the RFL brought in a psychologist from Huddersfield. He was giving us little exercises to do. He took us into a room where we were told to relax. Some players fell asleep because they were so relaxed... or bored. He told us all week that when we were under pressure during the game, he would play us some music and when we heard it, it would give us more energy and so on.

During the game, we were waiting for this music to come on; anyway it wasn't played at all. I'm not sure what happened. Something clearly went wrong. I had been given a tape by the psychologist that I was told to listen to when I had a quiet half hour. I was told that when listening to the tape I should shut my eyes, relax and think about all the positive things I had done in the game. I would sit there thinking about tries I had scored and so on. He said when I came to play, somewhere in my brain, I would take this onto the field with me. I had a good game that day, I was making good breaks and I set James Lowes up for a try.

Ettingshausen was my opposite centre and I was really causing him some problems. I know we lost but if we came off the field thinking we had done our best, that's all a coach can ask. I got a good write up from the Australian journalists who said I was one of the best players that day.

Great Britain versus Australia or New Zealand are the hardest games to play in. They are very quick, non-stop and there are not many gaps in the defence. When we get tackled by those guys, we know about it. I'm glad I was played in the centre and not in the pack. When I played for Great Britain, we seemed to be able to beat the Australians in one test, but never to win a series. I believe that when we won the first test, the second test came round and we thought: 'We've done it once, we can do it again'. There's something there that gives the players a false sense of security. The opposition, who have lost the first match, come into the second one really fired up. A test series is hard to handle mentally. The Australians have tough, high intensity games week in, week out. Our Super League competition is approaching that now.

My last international appearance was for Great Britain in the first Test against New Zealand on 31 October – Halloween - 1998. I scored, but we lost 22-16. I had a calf injury and didn't play for the rest of the series. The problem emanated from my back. I would run for 20 minutes and then suddenly, my calf would tighten up. It turned out I had a bulging disc that was hitting on a nerve in my back. That in turn was causing a problem in my calf.

Andy Goodway wanted me to have an injection in my thumb so I could go on the 1999 Tri Series tour down under. I played against Wakefield for Saints on 8 August. My thumb was pointing upwards; someone landed on it and smashed it backwards. All the tendons and ligaments in my thumb were knocked backwards. The next day, Great Britain had a training exercise in the Lake District. We were raft building and tree climbing - team building exercises. My thumb was very badly swollen, so I couldn't really do much and ended up just watching. Andy Goodway was alright. I liked him, he was down to earth and I could talk to him. He just said I should join in as best as I could. I was sent to see a specialist at Fairfield Hospital in St Helens. He told me I needed the ligaments strengthening with an operation. I asked him to do it after the season. I played on with a bad thumb and was booked straight in at the end of the season. Goodway said: 'You've been playing with it, it's only three games overseas. You can have your operation when we get back'. I told him I wanted it done straight away.

I had a chance of playing for Ireland in the 2000 World Cup. I got a phone call from the Irish coach, Steve O Neill who was working alongside Andy Kelly. I told him I would play for them as players were swapping countries through the grandparents' rule. It wasn't my granddad who was Irish though, it was my great granddad. They didn't seem worried about this. John Kear and David Howes rang me up to talk to me about playing for England and I told them I was playing for Ireland. They asked me if I could prove my Irish heritage. 'Of course I can', I lied. I thought 'these two are going to throw a spanner in the works'. I think that having turned down England, they would have made a big fuss with the RFL if I had played for Ireland. There would have been trouble. I sat down, thought about it and decided not to play. I would have loved to have played for Ireland, everybody seemed to be defecting from different countries.

I know people who played for Wales, not mentioning any names, and they are about as Welsh as a leprechaun. At times it was farcical. I know they've got to try and build up these sides somehow. I had played for England, so I thought it would be nice to get an Irish cap as it would make a set. It wasn't just that, I had been told by Chris Joynt that the Irish set up was a bit more relaxed than the English one. Luke Ricketson and Kevin Campion even came over from Australia to play for Ireland. I don't know if the RFL would have investigated my claim to be Irish-qualified. Joynty and I have been on trips to Ireland on a few occasions, Chris more than me as he has family over there. I like Ireland and have had some good times there. I would like to investigate my family tree and see how far I could take it back.

I announced my retirement from international rugby league in 2001 at the age of 29. I think it was the right time. I'd had enough of all the travelling and staying in hotels. I didn't ever really take to the international scene. Playing-wise it was good, but I found the set up cliquey. Coming into a camp when I played for Featherstone or even Bradford, there weren't many of my team mates there. I had to find someone who had a similar outlook to me and that's why I got on so well with Joynty.

Great Britain has been second best in the international rugby league pecking order for a long time now. New Zealand are also beating us at times. League has a good club game, but is not so strong internationally, while the reverse is true of rugby union.

## Deryck Fox played alongside Paul at Featherstone and Bradford and was on the 1992 Great Britain tour with him

*Deryck:* "My first memories of Paul are meeting him when he was a young lad at Featherstone, who Peter Fox thought was going to be a world beater. He hadn't come to the club highly recommended though; he just appeared on the scene. Peter had coached his father John in the 1970s and told us that Paul was going to turn out to be one of the best players we would see. Paul was very shy, he never really said anything, he just came in and did what he had to do. I was one of the main players at the club then and when Paul came along, it was nice to see fresh faced talent coming through. It was rare that we had special talent like Paul come to Featherstone Rovers. We had an influx of players into the club year after year, but Paul was something special. In training, he looked towards me, Paul Lyman and Alan Banks. We were players who were still young, around his age, people he could mix and associate with.

We were the first to come up with the ploy of looking one way and kicking the other for the team to score. It happened when we were playing Warrington, I was about to kick one way, changed my mind at the last minute to kick the other way for myself to chase and it paid off. Trevor Clark named the move 'ice cream'. I don't know why, it just came into his head. The move worked though.

I remember talking to Robin Whitfield who was a top referee then. He said it was very hard to referee the move regarding offside as the referee would be following play and looking towards where I would be running to and not at the players behind me. Paul used to read the move extremely well and I just used to pop the ball through to the corner for him.

A lot of players spoke to Paul to keep him going during the 1992 tour. He was the type of person who liked his home comforts. To be away from home for such a long time was hard for him. I think it helped having players such as me there who he could talk to. He knew he had close friends around him while he was away. I had been on tour in 1990 so knew what it was like. He was a young lad who missed home greatly.

When I left Featherstone I was at the turning point of my career, Featherstone had been in the Second Division. We got out of there back into the First Division. At 28-years-old, I had to make a move. I had come back from the 1992 tour as undefeated midweek team captain. I said to myself I had won no medals and never played in a major final. It wasn't the financial side of things that made me move to Bradford, but a desire to win medals. Paul joined a year later. I had been back to Featherstone to play against Paul and told him 'I'm going to get stick here'. I remember Paul's first game for Bradford back at Featherstone. As he had refused to play for Great Britain in the Sevens in Australia, the Rugby Football League had banned him from playing for his club side that weekend.  He came down with the players and I told him that the first penalty we got I would go for goal and I wanted him to bring the sand on. He said 'I'm not doing that, they'll lynch me'. I told him he should as it would be a bit of a laugh and he would hear what they were like at the far side of the field.

His wife and daughter were sat with my wife in the stand and the abuse our wives got that day was unbelievable. I'm not bothered on the playing side, but that was terrible. In fact, Adele took matters into her own hands and confronted somebody, put it this way, I don't think they'd say anything bad to her again.

We had some success the year Paul joined Bradford as we only lost the league to Wigan on points difference. We were growing in stature. The year Featherstone were relegated, Bradford only avoided joining them on points' difference. Peter Fox had joined Bradford, rebuilt the side and did a great job in getting Paul to come to the club. Paul brought a whole new dimension as we knew he could score a try from anywhere on the field. He was a major influence that season with the tries he scored.

He's been a credit to the game and himself. He helped me as well because wherever we were on the field I could rely on him to get us out of trouble. Paul could always get us a try. I loved playing in the same side as him. He was a great player."

Arriving at St Helens
(Photo: Bernard Platt)

# 5. Becoming a Saint

I began my St Helens career in the back of a van. I signed for them on 29 November 1995 and they organised a press conference where I had to jump out of a security van waving a Saints scarf with two security guards beside me. I just thought 'bloody hell', I didn't want to do it. I knew that Saints were a big club. I looked at the place, with the club shop and the ground behind it and was pleased to be there.

Kevin Ward had paved the way for the Yorkshire folk at St Helens. The supporters held him in high esteem; there was also Sonny Nickle who was a big Saints man, but was now going to Bradford as part of my transfer. The club was friendly and I soon settled in. People in the office, in the shop, Alan Gibbs who used to help Stan Wall, all of them were great. It's not just the players; it's everybody there who make the club what it is. People like Steph in the restaurant, she would always make us a brew. She would help the players because she loves the club. We had some lovely food up in the restaurant. We used to jokingly rip into John the chef, saying 'what slop have we got today John?' He used to pretend to scratch his big beard over the food in reply.

Stan Wall, the kit manager, has some stories. He used to tell us about his brother who was in the Home Guard during the Second World War. He would also tell us about his days as a referee. When I asked him to change my studs, he never used to like doing it for some reason. He would be huffing and puffing, maybe it was too much for him.

Another character in the dressing room was Stan's assistant Jack Coatsworth, better known as 'Toffee Jack'. He would always bring toffees in. He is a smashing fellow, he would do anything for us. He always used to call me 'cockle' and was always smiling. People like that behind the scenes should be mentioned because they are an important part of the club. Without them, the players wouldn't achieve half as much. They would work for nothing if needs be. People like them are at every club and it's nice to be able to give them some credit. At Featherstone, after training, Annie would make sandwiches for the players. She was a pensioner. Some players don't appreciate it, but there are others who stop and think and are grateful. At Bradford too, there were also hardworking people behind the scenes.

When I went to Knowsley Road as a Featherstone player we knew we were in for a hard game. Featherstone couldn't match St Helens at Knowsley Road. For the away team it wasn't a nice place to go. Having it as my home ground I thought was tremendous. The pitch is undoubtedly the best in the league, John the groundsman and Neil Holding before him have done excellent work on it. I had never really noticed, but it's on a bit of a hill. It's a big and wide playing surface. With three stands or covered terraced areas, it's closed in and the crowd generate a really good atmosphere. There has been talk of Saints leaving Knowsley Road but it has not happened yet. I think that the ground just needs improving a bit, but that costs a lot of money so it's difficult. There's history there that should not be lost.

I hadn't really done weight training until I came to Saints. I put some muscle on while at St Helens which was a good thing. As for the conditioning, it wasn't that much harder than what I had previously done. The defensive drills that we did were better though, we had to think about things a bit more. With the game changing, and going full-time, the coaching had to become more up to date.

When I was at Featherstone, I had my own place in the dressing room as did everyone else. If a new player came in and sat down he would be told that he couldn't sit there as that was someone's place and he'd been there some years. That's how it was for training; obviously for matches we would go where our numbers were. Soon after I joined St Helens there was a training session where I went into the home dressing room and got changed. It turns out I was in somebody's spot. I thought 'stuff this' and went to get changed in the away dressing room. A few more players ended up coming into the away dressing room to get changed for training. Joynty was one of them. We had our own little gang.

My first game for Saints was against Workington in the shortened Centenary Season at Knowsley Road on 3 December 1995. I slipped over the line in wet conditions and scored as Saints won 58-10. I gave a few good balls to Sully, but I didn't have the chance to make breaks myself. Again, I was a trying a bit too hard. It was a big task with that huge money tag on my head. I felt that all the attention was on me, but I think I handled it alright. Having the tag of the world's most expensive rugby league player never really bothered me that much. I had no control over it and just had to get on with playing. I didn't think about it, but it was a nice title to have.

I came to Saints in the middle of the Centenary Season, the last winter season before Super League started. My first derby against Wigan was the Regal Trophy Final on 13 January 1996 in front of a packed house at the McAlpine Stadium. I felt guilty playing in the game. I hadn't played in any of the previous rounds and I felt awful just playing in the final. I didn't think it was fair that I had taken somebody's spot who had played in the previous rounds. I scored a try in the corner, it was a touch-and-go game. It was very tense and the atmosphere was great. We lost 25-16, but people said it had been a classic final. Henry Paul scored a late try and that was it. As Wigan went to collect the trophy, our skipper Bobbie Goulding brought the Saints players together to talk to us, encouraging us to use the experience as a springboard for Super League. The teams for the final were:

*St Helens:* S. Prescott, J. Hayes, S. Gibbs, P. Newlove, A. Sullivan, K. Hammond, B. Goulding, A. Perelini, K. Cunningham, I. Pickavance, C. Joynt, S. Booth, D. Busby.
Subs: A. Northey, V. Matautia.
*Scorers:* Tries: Hayes, Newlove, Cunningham. Goals: Goulding (2).
*Wigan:* G. Connolly, J. Robinson, V. Tuigamala, K. Radlinski, M. Offiah, H. Paul, S. Edwards, N. Cowie, M. Hall, T. O'Connor, S. Quinnell, M. Cassidy, S. Haughton.
Subs: R. Smyth, M. Dermott.
*Scorers:* Tries: Paul (2), Tuigamala, Radlinski. Goals: Paul (4), drop-goal: Edwards.

The coach at the time was Eric Hughes. I liked Eric, he had a bit of a reputation for being a bit wild as a player and we could see that in the dressing room sometimes, he really got keyed up. There was a bit of aggression in him that he used to bring out in team talks. When we used to get a rub, he would rub us. Every player who got on the masseurs table would get a bit of a team talk in their ear from Eric along the lines of 'you're better than the opposition, be confident, get stuck into them'. He really got into it and really wanted to win. I found it good to be around him. But Eric's days were numbered when Shaun McRae came to the club and he left.

I found travelling to Lancashire a bit hard. I had never dreamt I would end up playing in Lancashire. In the past I thought that maybe I would sign for Leeds, Yorkshire's biggest club, but now I was driving to Lancashire. I thought 'what am I doing' but the transfer was done and dusted. I didn't realise I was going to be at

Saints for so long, I had signed a four year deal and thought that would be it. I was happy at the club though. I heard comments from Bradford supporters that I wouldn't stick it out at Saints. I would have stayed at Saints until I retired if I had been allowed to. The only bind was the travelling, but it just meant getting up early.

However, some mornings, I would be stuck in the traffic. Once when Shaun McRae was coach, the M62 was shut completely, a lorry carrying orange juice had been blown over and there was juice all over the carriageway. The police closed it down. I phoned in and explained that I couldn't get through and Shaun was fine about it. It was the same with Ian Millward later in my Saints career, if I phoned in and something like that happened that I couldn't do anything about, they were fine. All the coaches at Saints were sympathetic about my travelling. I wasn't late for training often. I do hate the M62 though. The furthest I go on it now is junction 26 for Bradford to see Carl Winterburn. Anything further than junction 26 and I don't want to know.

One thing the travelling did affect was socialising with the team. I couldn't be with them all the time. Sometimes I couldn't make it when they were going out. That's my one regret of living so far away; I was a little bit out of the way. But I did my fair share of socialising anyway.

Generally I would sit on my own on the coach for away games if there were enough seats. Sometimes I was picked up near my home depending on where we were playing. As long as I was on the coach before we arrived at the ground that was acceptable to the club.

Away from Knowsley Road, Headingley was one of my favourite grounds, with a fine playing surface and excellent changing rooms. My least favourite ground was Wilderspool, Warrington's old ground. Everything seemed bad: the changing rooms, the showers and the pitch seemed narrow as well with the snooker club on one side. Hull's old ground, the Boulevard was sometimes a bit unpleasant mainly due to the behaviour of some speccies. They used to have a cage type tunnel we walked through to get onto the pitch and some people would spit at us.

This also happened to me on occasions at Naughton Park in Widnes. Sometimes I felt like I wanted to do it back to them, but that would be wrong.

I have to say though, it was always good to hear the Hull fans belt out *Old Faithful* at the Boulevard. My dad and my uncle played there so I liked hearing it. It was especially strong when my uncle played there in the 1980s. Hull were the top side in the game then. Saints fans have their moments vocally though. Leeds have a good vocal section in the South Stand as well.

In 1996, the game switched to summer with the advent of Super League. Playing in summer has made the game quicker; the grounds are so much better because they're firm and fast, and better for a side-step.

I think one of the reasons we're catching up with Australia is that we're not playing in mud. What I used to wonder was why we didn't play all the games at night? I didn't like playing at 3.00pm in the middle of August as it was the hottest time of the day. Even with a 6.00pm kick off in the height of summer, the temperatures could still be quite high.

I really wanted the authorities to sort the kick off times out. I used to think the people who were in charge of rugby league had never played the game because if they had, they would realise what the players were going through. I felt that they were sitting in their offices making rules up and didn't have a clue about the players. Undoubtedly though, summer rugby has changed the face of rugby league.

The introduction of summer rugby also saw players at the top level becoming full-time professional for the first time. But during most of my career, in practice I was always a full-time professional. At Featherstone, I didn't have a job outside the game until the hospital porter one. What is true is that I had never trained full-time until I joined to St Helens.

But now things have swung the other way. Speaking to players at other clubs, the training schedules they had were ridiculous. The club might have them come in at 7.00am doing weights and keep them there all day. They only did that just to say that the players were full-time. Usually, I think it is possible to get all the training done in a morning.

The 1996 season opened with the Challenge Cup, and a fourth round tie at Castleford. I scored a hat trick as we started off the season in style, and I won the man-of-the-match award as well. I followed that with two tries at Rochdale the next week, and another two at Salford as we stormed into the semi-final. There we beat Widnes 24-14 at Wigan to reach Wembley, but I didn't score.

**1996 Challenge Cup Final: St Helens versus Bradford Bulls.**
Wembley. 27 April 1996. Won 40-32.

It was always my dream to play at Wembley and I can remember after Saints had beaten Widnes in the 1996 Challenge Cup semi-final, I was driving home and was asked: 'Are you pleased? You must be really pleased'. I said: 'No'. I was asked why and I told them: 'We haven't won it yet'. It was nice to get there, but on the day, I was very nervous. It is not something I could enjoy. It's a game of rugby league seen by more people than any other, beamed all across the world.

During the week of the final, BBC's *Grandstand* made a feature on me. It was a bit embarrassing as they wanted to film me during a team session in the swimming pool. They told me to act naturally, but I was conscious of the camera and I kept having a sly look at the camera. I felt a bit self-conscious.

We went down to train at Eton School. It's a different world there; people from my background never get into those places normally. The pupils came out to watch us train wearing their dickey bows and gowns. Prince William was there at the time and we were told that he was around somewhere. It was quite exciting and a lovely day. In the afternoon, we went to a boating clubhouse just off the Thames. They put a nice meal on for us and they had some electronic clay pigeon games for the lads to play on instead of us just sitting around. It was a good laugh. Also, we went out on a boat. It was scorching hot and the type of day where we would usually go for a couple of pints. However we had the small matter of the Challenge Cup Final the next day. Days like that are special, the players get looked after and the club tries to keep them relaxed.

It was tremendous walking out of the tunnel at Wembley. I couldn't see anything at first. I was standing in the tunnel, it was on an incline and as we came up all I could see were the Coca Cola signs at the other end. It levels out and then we were in the concertinaed tunnel that leads out onto the pitch. When we came out of that, BOOM, the noise hit us. The Saints speccies were at the tunnel end that day as well which made it even more special.

People always say that Wembley days go quickly and they're right. It did and I tried to remember it. I have the match on video, but to be honest I don't think I've watched it. The pitch itself is like any other piece of turf, but it's the surroundings that make it seem

In full flight against the London Broncos at Knowsley Road
(Photo: Bernard Platt)

Celebrating winning Super League in 1996
(Photo: Bernard Platt)

so much bigger. If players are used to playing on grounds with only one or two proper stands then Wembley, which seemed to envelop the pitch was something else. The roof went all the way round and it amplified the sound of the crowd. It's a shame Wembley was knocked down. It needed a lot of work doing to it, but the changing rooms were really good.

My first touch at Wembley was a pass to Sully that didn't go to hand. It didn't bother me too much although at the time I looked a bit of a fool. Something similar might happen in other games, but doing it on the big stage is nerve wracking. I remember Steve Prescott doing a massive dive for one of his two tries. A bit later I set up a try for Danny Arnold when I made a midfield break. Despite that, Bradford had a 14-12 lead at half time even though we had been 8-0 up at one point. Two points is nothing really in any game so we weren't too concerned. With 25 minutes left though, things had got worse, Robbie Paul had just gone over from close to the line and the score was 26-12 for Bradford. I thought it was all over in my heart of hearts. It was scorching hot and it looked like goodnight for us. Then three Bobbie Goulding bombs and three tries to Kieron Cunningham, Simon Booth and Ian Pickavance and we were back in the lead. All three bombs were virtually in the same position, it was unbelievable. They must have been gutted, especially Nathan Graham who was the Bradford full back. He is well known for that match now.

Our comeback is the biggest ever in a Challenge Cup Final. People said it was one of the best finals of all time and it was the first time in 20 years that Saints had won the cup. None of that meant anything to me on the pitch during the game though, I simply didn't think of things like that. I dropped to my knees at the final hooter, glad it was all over. I just looked up to the sky and said 'Thank you'. I was just so happy and relieved. We had been under pressure and concentrating for 80 minutes, then all of a sudden the hooter goes and as we had won, we could let it all go. With a packed house of nearly 80,000 there, it was an amazing experience. We were all jumping on each other. We got into a huddle and Bobbie started talking to us. It's something he used to do in big games as our captain. I can't remember what he said, maybe it was just 'well done'.

I had to pinch myself going up the famous steps. In later years when Joynty was captain he used to make me laugh. Every time we won a Challenge Cup or a Grand Final he came over to me and would say: 'Make sure you're directly behind me on the steps, you'll be in the photos in all the papers tomorrow'. I would never have thought of that. That's a good bit of advice from Chris and from that day, I always tried to be second in the queue so I could be in some good photos.

We lifted up a sign saying 'It's for you' to our supporters. I think it was David Howes's idea. It was a nice thing to be able to do for the speccies. It made the day a bit more special for them. We went round on the lap of honour on the running track. We got to the Bradford end, and there was a surge of people towards me. They were not there to congratulate me. I just showed them my medal. They were mad, but it didn't get out of hand. The next day we went back to St Helens to travel through the town on an open top bus to go to the town hall. It was lashing down with rain but there were thousands of people on the streets. We travelled back from London in our sportswear and stopped at a service station to get changed into our suits. I was at the front on the bus and I had a skinhead haircut then as the pictures show. I was getting squashed in the corner. Maybe the suits had shrunk as it rained so much that day. It was a great day though.

People have said to me that when we win things the trophy gets passed round from pillar to post and it must have an effect. It does. The Challenge Cup itself was dented. The two angels on either side were both loose. Everyone gets a hold of it in the hotel after the game. My dad's name is on it - all the captains are on it. In my opinion, it is a very good trophy, one of the best in sport really. As for the Super League trophy, there is a big dent in the side of that from when a St Helens player dropped it.

We were staying in Windsor and after the game, a few of the single lads visited a couple of pubs and then decided to head back to the hotel to see what the rest of us were doing. They asked a policeman for directions to the nearest taxi rank, he recognised them from the television coverage and arranged for a police van to take them back to the hotel. They travelled in the van and as a wind up organised for the police to go into the hotel and tell David Howes and Eric Ashton that the players had been arrested.

I like Eric, he is 'old school', very much a Lancastrian version of Foxy. He was panicking when he heard this, at which point the Saints players jumped out of the van and yelled 'surprise'.

Joynty won a man-of-the-match trophy that day, and I thought it wasn't the best trophy. It was on a square of marble and I thought it looked like an ashtray. He left it on the table while we were sitting around. I lit a cigar and kept on flicking my ash into Joynty's trophy. He didn't notice what I was doing. He finally realised and went mad with me.

*Saints:* Prescott, Arnold, Gibbs, Newlove, Sullivan, Hammond, Goulding, Perelini, Cunningham, Leathem, Joynt, Booth, Northey.
Subs: Hunte, Martyn, Matautia, Pickavance.
*Scorers:* Tries: Prescott 2, Arnold 2, Cunningham, Booth, Pickavance, Perelini. Goals: Goulding 4.
*Bradford:* Graham, Cook, Calland, Loughlin, Scales, Bradley, Paul, Hamer, Dwyer, McDermott, Donougher, Nickle, Knox.
Subs: Medley, Fairbank, Donohue, Hassan.
*Scorers:* Tries: Scales, Paul 3, Dwyer. Goals: Cook 6.

In my younger days at Featherstone
(Photo: David Williams)

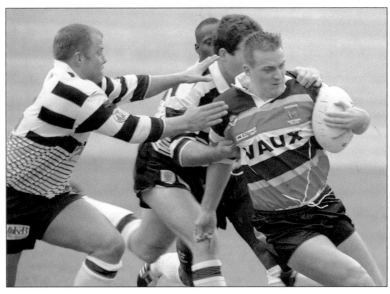

Playing for Bradford Northern (Photos: David Williams)

Playing for St Helens in the 2001 Challenge Cup Final
(Photo: David Williams)

With Chris Joynt at the 2001 Challenge Cup Final
(Photo: David Williams)

Playing for England in the 1995 World Cup (Photo: David Williams)

Ready to tour Australia and New Zealand for Great Britain in 1992
(Photo: David Williams)

Battling it out with the Australians for Great Britain
(Photos: David Williams)

End of the road: My last game – for Castleford against Salford
(Photo: David Williams)

# 6. Winning Super League

After our triumph at Wembley, the rest of the season was the battle for the first Super League title.

The first Super League game to take place at Knowsley Road was, fittingly, against Wigan. We beat them 41-26 after they had taken an early lead. It was a warm day and I did a lot of work in defence. Wigan seemed to be shifting the ball to my side of the field and I tackled well. I tackled Andy Farrell more times than anyone else that game. Success is not all about scoring great tries; it's sometimes about work in defence. Everyone at Saints went crazy after the game, it was a party atmosphere. I thought: 'what's happening here?' I've played in derbies for Featherstone and Bradford, but a Saints versus Wigan derby is something different, a step up. Saints fans were so happy to beat Wigan and loved shouting 'Wigan walk' to the Wigan supporters as they would head for the exits early if they lost.

The players got wrapped up in it. The Wigan players weren't used to losing and they were upset. It was brilliant to upset them. But I wouldn't say that the games were enjoyable experiences. Before the game, I would be nervous and concentrating on the game ahead. The crowds were unbelievable and the atmosphere was so intense. The only time the players enjoy it is when we have got a good result. That's when it sinks in, the directors are happy and as long as they're happy everybody else at the club is happy. The supporters are over the moon, it's often been said if we lost every other game, but beat Wigan they'd be happy, but deep down I'm sure they wouldn't be.

When I first played against Bradford for Saints in 1996, the Bulls fans really gave it to me. Standing behind the posts, especially at the Eddington end at Knowsley Road, where the fans are really close to the players, we could hear abuse – or support – from the crowd. At Odsal, there was the speedway track between the sticks and the supporters so we didn't hear as much.

Another stand out moment that year was the week before Wembley when we played Halifax away and I scored another hat trick. Everybody was playing poorly and the hat trick won us the game 30-28.

It's been said that I never showed much emotion on the field, but that's how I am. If someone scored a try I congratulated them, but I didn't get carried away with dance routines and so on. When Martin Offiah used to score, people thought that he used to take the mickey out of the opposition. That meant that when their players got hold of him they wanted to crack him.

Having said that, in Australia they have produced a video of the best try celebrations; some of them are quite funny and inventive. There's one where a team line up like bowling pins, one player rolls the ball at them and they all wobble and fall over. I've never seen a team do something like that; surely it must get the opposition's goats up.

I used to be first off the pitch at Saints. The reason was that there was only a tankful of hot water at the club and if the away team got to the showers first, they got it all. It always seemed that when the hooter went I was on the side of the pitch where the changing rooms are as very often in the second half Saints would play towards the restaurant end. I wouldn't hang about as I didn't really like staying on the pitch after the game, but I would clap the speccies sometimes.

We had some close escapes during the 1996 Super League season. Castleford away on 2 August is one match that the supporters still talk about. Jason Flowers looked certain to score a try that would have taken the game away from Saints, but somehow Steve Prescott and Joey Hayes brought him down. We hung on to win 20-16, and I got one of our tries.

The battle for the first Super League title was very tight throughout the season. We just concentrated on the games, and don't realise at the time how much these incidents could change the whole season. We didn't realise how close we were to missing out. It could have been so different. Once our opponents broke our line, it was all about how good our scrambling defence was. Thankfully we had pace in the backs. Steve Prescott at full back played very well. Under a high ball, he was safe as houses.

Another close call was the game at London the week before our visit to Castleford, where Apollo Perelini's late try won us the game 32-28 after a long deliberation by the video referee. I scored in the first half, but then got injured and was on the bench. I couldn't see if it was a try from where I was sitting. All the lads on the bench were debating whether we were going to be given the try or not. I just sat quiet and still, hoping and praying that it would be given. Apollo took a few of the Broncos over the line with him, for him to still have got the ball down took amazing strength. He played really well for Saints and is one of the nicest guys you could wish to meet. I don't know how he got that ball down, but he's very religious and maybe that helped him.

When a decision on a try goes to the video referee, a player often knows if he hasn't really scored. Sometimes the ball has been touched down just short or something else has happened. The ref 'goes to the screen' and if I don't think I've scored, I just think 'no chance' and walk away. All the lads jump up and down and pat me on the back and I would tell them 'I haven't scored'. They would say 'let's watch it on the screen' and I would insist I hadn't scored.

I used to have a shocking relationship with referees; I used to blow up at them if decisions went against me. Towards the end of my career I changed. Then every time a decision went against me or against Saints I would just keep my mouth shut and get on with it. I felt better because referees never change their decisions. I would still shout at the touch judges occasionally. I think they should have more responsibility and authority. If they see a foul, they should come on with their flag. At the moment, in my opinion, sometimes it seems as if they're just stood out there catching the sun. They can often see if someone is swinging an arm and if the referee misses it they should get on the pitch to show an offence has happened.

Coming towards the end of the season, we were only a point ahead of Wigan and knew we couldn't afford to drop a single point. We played Warrington at home on the last day of the season and we had to win to take the Super League title. It was like a final that day. Everyone was up for it; our forwards were brilliant. From the kick off, it was clear how determined we were. Everything we touched that day seemed to turn to gold. I scored a couple of tries. I remember that Anthony Sullivan saved a certain try. Richard Henare was over the line about to put the ball down and Sully raced back to knock the ball out of his hands. That was unbelievable. It wasn't just about attack for us in 1996, it was about defence too. We only lost twice in Super League, at Wigan and Bradford. However, Wigan did beat us in the Premiership Final at Old Trafford.

It was great lifting the first Super League trophy even though I don't like the design of the trophy. That wasn't important though. The prestige of us being champions was all I cared about, it had been a long season. To win it in front of our speccies was great as well. If we'd have won it away from Knowsley Road, our speccies would still have been there, but doing it at our home ground was something special. It was a wonderful day. I don't know if the night was wonderful because I can't remember it. The top two places were:

Stones European Super League 1996

|  | Played | For | Against | Points |
|---|---|---|---|---|
| 1. St Helens | 22 | 950 | 455 | 40 |
| 2. Wigan | 22 | 902 | 326 | 39 |

I ended up with 36 tries in 27 matches that season; I was playing in a good side. I was always top try scorer at Featherstone and they weren't nearly as good as St Helens, so it followed that I would cross the line more with Saints. It was easier for me being surrounded by quality players throughout the side.

There have been some celebrations at Knowsley Road since 1996 with all the Challenge Cup and Grand Final wins and remembering them is often hampered by the amount of beer we put away. Sometimes we had such a good drink we must have resembled Thunderbird puppets, it looked like someone was working us as we babbled away talking broken biscuits. Sometimes I would go straight home after the game and come back to St Helens the next day if the club had organised a homecoming at the ground.

Taking the double from Wigan in 1996 was a big thing. David Howes rang me up a while back and said he wanted to thank me. I asked him what for and he said that when I came to St Helens, that was when things started happening for the club. We won the double the first year and it went on from there. I said thanks to him. It wasn't just me though; it was the whole Saints team who broke the Wigan dynasty. To deny them after they had dominated British rugby league for all those years was a big achievement. Saints were always knocking on the door, but as the saying went they were 'always the bridesmaid and never the bride'. It turned round from 1996 and now Saints are ahead of Wigan.

After we had won the Super League title, we reached the Premiership final at Old Trafford. We faced Wigan at Old Trafford, and lost 44-14. I scored early on to put us ahead. It was the 250th try of my career, but by half time we were 18-8 down. Towards the end of the game I injured my hamstring which ruled me out of the Great Britain tour to the South Pacific.

A highlight of 1996 was setting the record for scoring in most successive games in Super League after I scored in nine consecutive games. My run started at Leeds on 8 April, and continued until our win at Sheffield on 8 June. I missed out against Workington the next week, and then scored in another seven consecutive games. I'm still joint-holder of that record.

Until 2004, I held the record for most tries in a Super League season with 28 in 22 games in the same season. Kris Radlinski was close to the record one year, but he broke his wrist and couldn't play in the last game. He'd been great that season, scoring left, right and centre, but luckily for me, the record was safe for another year. The record stayed with me for eight years then Leeds half back Danny McGuire broke it. I presented McGuire with a trophy for breaking my record. Joynty rang me and asked if the rep from Tetley's could ring me as they wanted me to do the presentation. I said 'no problem' and went down to Headingley to give Danny the plate. They didn't do anything similar when I got the most tries in 1996. He got the record equalling try against St Helens which was a little ironic. But then in the last round of the season, he missed Leeds' game through injury, and Bradford Bulls winger Lesley Vainikolo overtook his tries total to finish as top try scorer.

In December, being invited to the BBC Television *Sports Personality of the Year* award shows was always a highlight. The 1996 one was best for me because it was the first I went to. It was all fresh to me. Joynty, Sully and Precky and I went down for Saints that year. It was brilliant. We flew to London and stayed in a top hotel with all the other sports personalities. Evander Holyfield was there, there were famous sports people there. To be up close to them was exciting. But I find parts of the show boring, it goes on for two hours and rugby league gets about five seconds coverage, other sports with less support getting far more.

After the programme and the formalities, there was a free bar and disco. Over the years, I saw different famous people from sport there. Some didn't drink and some behaved themselves such as Michael Owen who left quite soon after the show. We had a good time with Tom Docherty, the snooker player, and Dickie Bird. We got talking to him. He's from Barnsley and he was saying 'you rugby lads are brilliant not like the footballers, the Liverpool players wouldn't even talk to me'. I told him I was from Yorkshire. We said: 'Go on Dickie, give us the finger' in the hope he would give us the famous umpiring signal for 'out'. He had a good crack with us.

We also spoke to Stephen Hendry. He was alright. We got talking to the rugby union guys as well, Jeremy Guscott is a nice fellow as is Matt Dawson. We also had a good chat with footballer, Dion Dublin. They were all nice lads. Some I didn't dare approach. I wanted to go and talk to Gary Lineker, I think he knew who we were because he is pretty clued up on sport. I didn't know what to say to him though.

We took Andy Leathem one year and the disco shut so we went back to our hotel. Andy got a big round of drinks in, and was carrying them on a tray. We could see he wasn't comfortable holding it and he ended up spilling them all. It must have cost him £30 or £40. The cry went up: 'Get 'em back in Gripper'. He was gutted. That was the year we ended up with James Cracknell and Tim Foster, the Olympic rowers. They were students. Brendan Foster, the athletics commentator, knew a bit about rugby league. I was talking to him about the game one time. It was good to meet them all.

## Mal Kay was a St Helens director when Paul joined the club

"We had an inkling that Gary Connolly was going to leave the club. He was in Australia and there was feedback coming from there that a deal had been done between Gary and Wigan. Both Tom Ellard and I spoke to Gary on the phone, had lengthy conversations with him and every time we increased our offer to him we felt he moved the goalposts. Eventually, we realised that we were wasting our time. We had a feeling before then that he would go to Wigan. Maybe it was inevitable that we would lose him because at that time Wigan could afford to pay more to players than Saints. We had spoken to Paul Newlove hoping to bring him to the club as a like-for-like replacement for Connolly. We had been speaking to Paul for several months. However, we couldn't do a deal then.

A couple of years later, Saints got through to the Alliance Challenge Cup Final, to be played at Knowsley Road against Bradford. That night, Eric Hughes came upstairs to me and said that he had heard a whisper that Paul Newlove would be available from Bradford. The deal didn't materialise at that time as the negotiations for Super League were ongoing then. We kept in touch with Paul though and to be fair to Peter Fox, he told Paul that if he was to leave Bradford, the club he should go to was St Helens. He felt that our style of play would suit Paul and the club would look after him. Eric Hughes was adamant that Newlove would make the difference to the already good side we had assembled at the club.

Negotiations for him went on for a long time and were very difficult. Eric Ashton was a great supporter of him, Tom Ellard did a lot of work in negotiations and worked closely with me on the deal. Brian Smith was doing most of the negotiations for Bradford. We were up against a brick wall. He was adamant over the Saints players he wanted in exchange for Paul. He wouldn't do the deal unless we gave up those players. It was upsetting having to let those players leave as we were intent on strengthening the side rather than letting players go. Everybody felt that this signing was the one that mattered and would make the difference for us. All the Board chipped in to help pay for the deal as did some supporters. I don't think the club has looked back since we signed him. We've had some great players at the club over the years, but Paul is one of the finest signings the club has made. He was a major part of the jigsaw for our success since 1995.

People from Yorkshire told us that he wouldn't settle, he wouldn't come to training and that he would be moody. What we found though was that he was ultra professional. The coaching staff and everyone involved with the club would say 'we wish we had 20 players like him'. His attitude was spot on. If Paul had any problems, someone who knew him well would sit with him, find out what was wrong and iron things out.

The one thing that no-one ever took into account with Paul, but opposition players and coaches would say is that while everybody looked at Paul's attacking flair, defensively he was one of the best in the business. On top of that, Paul Newlove didn't need to touch a ball. He just needed to be on the field, once the play was coming over to his side of the field; defences would panic watching Newlove and would take dummy after dummy meaning that other players did well down that side of the field. Eric Hughes highlighted this strength of having him in the team.

People often wonder what Paul Newlove is like as a person. He is a very honest lad. He will always play straight by you, but if you let him down, that's it. There are no second chances. He is straightforward and that is why he rarely spoke to the press. People would think he might be having a go at someone; he wasn't, he was just telling it the way he saw it. If it upsets people, hard lines. If people speak to him, all they will get is the truth.

He's a shy and quiet lad, but deep down the feeling he has for the St Helens spectators is immense. It has come out of him more and more. Now that he has retired, it has started soaking in. He's never been one for running over to the spectators and clapping because he is shy. He got criticised heavily for that at other clubs, but Saints speccies took him to their hearts and understood him more. He is very appreciative of the Saints speccies. In turn, nobody at the club had a bad word for him."

# 7. Jason Johnson's holiday

1997 started off with us drawn against Wigan in the Challenge Cup at Knowsley Road. Bobbie Goulding was sent off just before half time, yet with 12 men we managed to secure a famous 26-12 victory. I was among our try scorers in the second half. There was a bit of a running battle between me and Andy Farrell all game. I don't know what I did but I seemed to upset him that day. I think it knocked him off his game.

At the end of the game as we were walking off the pitch, referee Russell Smith walked between us to keep things calm. I hung about for a bit and then went in. When players lose it's hard to take and people react in different ways. I haven't had any problems with him since, and we've played together for Great Britain.

The game is also known for when Derek McVey, who had been substituted in the second half, was interviewed live on BBC by Richard Duckenfield during the game. He came out with the classic 'people thought we were a one year shot, but f... ing hell we're still here aren't we?' Shocked silence from the commentary team – it was priceless. Anyway, it was a good, hard win. I was interviewed after the game and managed not to turn the airwaves blue. I did say the game had been quite tough, especially towards the end. As the hooter approached, it seemed as if Wigan were trying to give us a dig in every tackle. We just responded 'What's the score?' It was pure guts and determination that took us through that day.

In the next round we beat Hull 54-8 at Knowsley Road, and I got a hat trick. I scored again in our win at Keighley in the next round, but missed out in the semi-final against Salford. Our 50-20 win took us back to Wembley to face the Bradford Bulls again.

**1997 Challenge Cup Final: St Helens versus Bradford Bulls.**
Wembley. 3 May 1997. Won 32-22.

Bobbie was suspended for his high tackle on Neil Cowie in the win against Wigan. Lee Briers stepped in to take his place for the remaining cup rounds. He was only young, and was skinny. He didn't look like a rugby player; he looked like he would have trouble tackling a hot dinner. To be fair to him, he played well. He played in the semi-final against Salford, but Bobbie was back for the final and I felt for Lee. It's a tough one, because he played in most of the rounds, and the coach has to decide: 'Does Lee get the nod, but then do I deny Bobbie the chance of playing at Wembley?' We got the result again though and that's the main thing, it's what's good for the team that matters.

Bradford had tight jerseys for the final. They were skin tight yellow tops. It was a fresh idea, we couldn't grab them by their shirts to tackle them. We could see the bellies on their chunkier players though. It wasn't flattering for some of them. England did the same thing in rugby union. It's another trend that Bradford started. We went into half time in the lead this time, 16-10. At the start of the second half Bradford attacked us and I managed to pull off a try-saving tackle on Abi Ekoku. I dragged him back from scoring. I don't know how I did it because he was massive, strong and a good athlete. I remember watching the replay of the game on Sky that night in my hotel room after a few beers and I got some praise from Stevo.

Later on in the second half, I made a break and thought I was going to get a try. Sonny Nickle came from nowhere, he got hold of me and I thought he broke his arm making the tackle. In 1999 when he rejoined Saints he told me his arm had broken as he stopped me from scoring. He had just come back from a broken arm, so it might not have healed fully. I could see the whitewash in front of me and was very close to scoring.

We pulled away to 30-10 in the second half, so it wasn't as tense as the previous year's final. Tommy Martyn tackled Abi Ekoku. Abi didn't know what had hit him. He woke up with grass in his mouth. He dropped the ball and Chris Morley went in under the sticks, but it was disallowed as Tommy was penalised for the tackle.

I was playing opposite Danny Peacock. He was a tricky player to play against. He had an awkward running style, sort of hunched up with his knees and arms lifted high. He ran a good angle and was strong as well. I had to be switched on defensively for the full 80 minutes when I played against him. Winning two Wembley finals in two years was a great feeling. Before I joined St Helens I remember thinking: 'Am I going to get a Wembley Challenge Cup Final?' Some really good players have never played in a Wembley final, Jeff Grayson comes to mind as one. I achieved what I wanted to do and there was more to come after the first. It wasn't as hot the second time round. It was an overcast day which suited me.

At Wembley, we knew what to expect more the second time round. We knew the layout of the changing rooms and so on. It still gives the players a buzz though. Playing at Wembley was always a pleasure.

Bobbie stood aside at the top of the steps to let Joynty lift the cup as he had skippered the side through the previous rounds; it was a nice gesture from him. Coming down the steps, people have said that I made a big display of emotion at someone off camera. It was to Mal Kay and Tom Ellard.

*St Helens:* Prescott, Arnold, Haigh, Newlove, Sullivan, Martyn, Goulding, O'Neill, Cunningham, Perelini, Joynt, McVey, Hammond.
Subs: Matautia, Pickavance, Northey, Morley.
*Scorers:* Tries: Martyn 2, Joynt, Sullivan, Hammond. Goals: Goulding 6.
*Bradford:* Spruce, Ekoku, Peacock, Loughlin, Cook; Bradley, Paul, McDermott, Lowes, Reihana, Nickle, Dwyer, McNamara.
Subs: Tomlinson, Medley, Knox, Calland.
*Scorers:* Tries: Peacock, Loughlin, Tomlinson, Lowes. Goals: McNamara 3.

We weren't as consistent in Super League as in 1996, and finished third. But one new competition this season was a World Club Championship involving all the Super League clubs in Britain, Australia and New Zealand. In June, we played Auckland, Cronulla and Penrith at Knowsley Road, losing all three matches. So we knew the return fixtures in July would be tough.

Staying in Coogee for the overseas leg of the tournament in 1997 was great, apart from having to play of course. The Holiday Inn hotel was right on the beach in a brilliant spot. It was just a taxi ride away from Sydney. It was fantastic place to spend three weeks. But Andy Leathem, the Saints prop, had a bit of a nightmare there. Gripper is a nice lad, but had the misfortune of being bitten by a spider. On 21 July we played Cronulla and I scored. We lost 28-12, an improvement on our 40-point defeat at Knowsley Road. Andy had a superb game. Despite only being a young lad, he really stood up to the punishment that the Cronulla pack threw his way. However, after that game, we were training on a playing field and Andy felt a bite on his leg. He didn't think anything of it, but it got worse and became swollen and infected. He went to the doctor and it turned out that the very rare White Tip Spider had bitten him. There had only been about five people in Australia to have been bitten by this spider and Gripper was one of them.

The wound was eating his leg away. He had a big hole in it. He didn't play for the next couple of weeks. That was typical of the luck he went through in his career with injuries. All the other players were taking the mickey out of him over the spider bite for the rest of the trip.

The next game saw us play Auckland Warriors who smashed us 70-6. Every time they scored a Maori banged a drum. He must have been exhausted by the final hooter. Before the game, most of the Saints players decided to get their hair dyed blonde. Looking back, it was a stupid idea. One did it and others copied him. The Australian commentators had a field day over it. The lads didn't ask me to go blonde, which was just as well as I wouldn't have done it.

While we were in New Zealand, Carl Hall's family looked after me. They took me and Joynty up in a police helicopter through one of their family who works for the police. We flew all over Auckland, it was superb. They took me to a rugby pub as well. We went in the back room and it was full of heavy biker Maoris. I thought we could be in trouble as they looked round at us; all I could think about was the film *Once were Warriors*. Nothing was said though.

We qualified for the latter stages of the tournament through points' difference after a Sean Long try against Penrith, a game that we lost narrowly 32-26. We played well that night and should have won. It was a good trip, but rugby got in the way. Maybe we saw it as a holiday. Saints then beat Paris St Germain 42-4 to qualify for a quarter final away to the Brisbane Broncos in October. I nearly didn't make it. The motorway was packed the day we were set to fly out. I left home at 6.00am, giving myself two hours to get to Saints for an 8.00am departure from the ground. Not only was the motorway very busy that day, but so was the East Lancs Road. I kept looking at my watch thinking that I wasn't going to make it in time. I got to the club and the coach had gone. I turned round and went back down the East Lancs Road, to try to find my way to Manchester Airport. I got lost. I know how to get to the airport from Yorkshire, but I didn't have a clue starting from St Helens. I had to get back on the M62 so I could find my route to the airport. The next thing was, I couldn't get off the M62 and was heading the wrong way, so had to turn round at a service station. I was on my mobile phone to David Howes during all of this. They organised for my car to be parked for me away from the airport. I ran into the airport and the woman on the desk asked: 'Are you Mr Newlove?' I said I was and got the reply: 'You've missed your flight'.

I wouldn't go on my own. I didn't want to fly all that way without someone to talk to. First of all, the club tried to get Joynty off the plane when they stopped in Amsterdam, so that he could fly back to Manchester and accompany me on the flight. They couldn't do it without taking his bags off as well so it was a non-starter. The club then arranged for academy player Jason Johnson to fly with me. He met me at the airport. We flew from Manchester to London, then to Hong Kong to meet the rest of the team.

I got to Hong Kong and prepared myself for a right rollicking and a big fine. Shaun McRae never said a word though; he took the mickey a bit as the rest of the lads did, but apart from that, I didn't get shouted at or anything. Jason Johnson came out of the whole commotion better than anyone. He didn't have to play and was in his element. He was out every night enjoying himself and had a good week. It was lovely and sunny in Brisbane and he was there, with sunglasses and Hawaiian shirts on, loving life. And to cap it all, we lost the game 66-12.

Another new experience in 1997 was playing a home game against Castleford at Liverpool FC's famous Anfield ground. The club were trying to generate some interest in rugby league in Liverpool. We won 42-16 and I scored two tries.

I thought the changing rooms were a bit old fashioned compared to Old Trafford. They weren't derelict or anything, but I thought there was a bit of wear and tear. The Liverpool fans in the Saints team were made up to be playing there. The big contrast in the ground was that at one end you had the marvellous Kop and the other was a small basic stand. The playing surface was good and it was enjoyable to play there.

A less happy experience in 1997 was trying to resolve some problems I had with Super League. Fortunately, Peter Fox was there in my corner when I had big trouble securing the loyalty bonus I was due from the ARL-Super League war. Everyone else was getting their bonus and I wasn't. The loyalty bonus was just for playing in this country and not signing for the ARL. I signed to Super League for the loyalty bonus because it was a lot of money and because I wanted to play in this country. I eventually ended up signing for St Helens. Mally Kay really fought for me, as did Eric Ashton. Saints got a top solicitor to help me. I eventually got paid, but it was after a couple of years and it was £20,000 short of what I was expecting. All the other players had got their bonus in a lump sum, but with me they split it into instalments. I was just pleased to get it after all the hassle.

I remember playing in the Challenge Cup semi-final at Central Park in 1997 against Salford. One of the leading RFL officials came into the changing room, all the lads were celebrating, there was beer flying everywhere. I saw him come in and I just sat there with my head down. He asked me what was up. I said: 'You know what's up'. All the room went quiet. I went on: 'You should give me my money, you've given it to all the other players, you owe me this money' and I ripped into him in front of everyone. After that, things got moving and I got my money. As soon as he left the changing room, I looked up and started celebrating with the boys. I'd got it off my chest. That dispute was also the reason I was reluctant to be interviewed by Sky at that time.

The 1997 season finished with us in the Premiership Final again at Old Trafford. In a repeat of the 1996 match, we faced Wigan again. I scored from 40 yards out in the first half, to make the score 14-8. But they beat us 33-20. I was put on report by Stuart Cummings for a high tackle, but the disciplinary committee took no further action against me.

In 1998, our defence of the Challenge Cup took us to Featherstone. It meant playing against my brother Richard. The press did a little interview with the pair of us before the game. He was playing on the opposite side of the field to me that day. We won 56-24, with 10 tries, but I didn't score. I got a better reception from the fans than when I went back with Bradford, they didn't boo me as much. A long time had passed since I left the club. It was a good crowd that day at Post Office Road, 2,759, Featherstone's biggest of the season, so the atmosphere was electric. Richard and I didn't really come into contact with each other much during the game which I suppose was a relief. The game was a 'David and Goliath' affair with us winning comfortably. I missed the last couple of minutes of the game. Their winger was only a little 'un and I ran into him and thought 'he's going to get it'. He tackled me and was quite feisty, I tried to head butt him, but didn't do a good job on him. As other players came in to complete the tackle, my arms were held. He landed on top of me and caught me just above my eye. I had a gash in it that needed about eight stitches, I still have a little bit of a scar to this day. All my team mates were laughing at me after the game, saying that I had been beaten up by a little winger.

1998 was the first Super League season that finished without Saints winning a trophy. Wigan knocked us out of the Challenge Cup in the sixth round, and Leeds beat us in the play-offs after we had beaten Bradford and Halifax.

It was also Shaun McRae's last season as coach. Our main game plan was to work the ball right and then shift it back left to Joynty, Sully and me. Sully ended the season as top try scorer for Saints with 26, so the plan must have worked. I scored 19 tries and Joynty got nine. In some games though, I found myself shut down a lot. If teams know what the opposition are going to do before the game starts, it's easier for them to cope with. That's how I felt. But then I moan when I'm not getting the ball so I can't have it both ways. However, sometimes I felt that the side could be doing something different instead of doing the same moves over and over again.

As a coach, Shaun McRae is a good talker. He explains the game well when he is on television. He had his ideas and he was successful at St Helens, Gateshead and Hull. Sometimes I thought he was a bit laid back. He didn't do much running about, but just watched training. One day at Saints, we were out on the training paddock and it was a really stormy day. We were doing a conditioning session, hitting the tackle bags and Shaun was watching from inside the club shop. We were getting muddy and wet through. He just said what has to be said. But, to be fair, we did win three trophies with him as coach.

One of our forwards had the reputation of not being the most enthusiastic trainer in the world. One time, there was something going wrong at Saints and we had a meeting to sort it out. More than a few eyebrows were raised when he piped up with 'you're not fit enough'. Everyone looked round at him because he was often at the back in training. At the back end of my career I encountered two players at Castleford similar to him on their approach to training. They would pull out of things if it got a bit too hard for them. I would shake my head and think: 'You wouldn't get away with that at a top club'. That's the difference between a side at the top of the league and one at the bottom.

Bobbie Goulding left Saints in 1998. He had been club skipper since the start of Super League and was our main playmaker and goalkicker. The incident that finished him at the club happened when Saints played Wigan in an 'On the Road' Super League game in Swansea in July 1998. We lost 36-2 with the only memorable incident for Saints being when trainer Nigel Ashley Jones was hit by Sky's moving camera. He was coming on the field and was in the way of the camera, which moves at around 30 miles an hour. It sent him up in the air and put him on his back, winded and motionless for a minute or two. I didn't see it and only found out about it after the game. Anyway, we went back to the hotel after the game and I went to bed. A few players stayed up drinking in the bar. The next morning we heard that Bobbie had said something to Anthony Sullivan.

I think that was the nail was in the coffin for Bobbie. Not long after, he left the club. I don't know what happened leading up to that night in Swansea and whether that was the last straw or not. I do remember him being very angry with Shaun McRae when he was dropped once. But things got sorted out and he was soon back in the side.

The fans loved Bobbie at St Helens, and used to sing: 'Walking in a Goulding wonderland' to him. He was a really good player, captain and goalkicker. When I first joined the club, he would run across the face of the defence giving me little drop-off balls.

I've always got on with Bobbie. He could get a bit silly at times, it's what you do off the field as well as on the field that counts. I feel that he missed his way, and it was a pity he left the club.

I was approached to go to Leicester and play rugby union. When I had a year left on my contract at Saints. I met Phil Larder at Brighouse Forte Hotel and we had a good meeting. He was keen as mustard to get me there and put me into the England set up. They were looking for players for the 1999 World Cup. I would have played my club rugby at Leicester with the RFU subsidising my wages. I said: 'Yeah, it sounds alright', but apparently it would have been too expensive for them to have bought out my contract at Saints, so they never went through with it. The money they were offering was a lot more than there was in league. I'd imagine Jason Robinson must have a good contract. If I had gone I would have played centre. I'm not that clear on the difference between outside and inside centre in union. The inside centre is generally a crash-ball-man while the outside centre has to have a bit more pace. I wouldn't have fancied the crash-ball-man job, so it would have been outside centre for me I think.

I played the sport at school and that is as far as I got as I played league instead. I was like anybody else from a league background, and believed that union was slow and boring to

82

watch, and was all kicks. I think that was true at the time, however the international scene is getting better. Their club game doesn't interest me.

I was amongst the first people to find out that Ellery Hanley would be coaching Saints in 1999. Chris Joynt and I both got phone calls to come to the club. Chris was our skipper; I don't know why they called me, I'm no good at representing players. Anyway, we got there and in the boardroom were Ellery and his agent. Everyone was shaking hands and congratulating Ellery on joining the club. We were the first players to meet him. It was definitely a surprise for everybody. His record stands for itself, he's done it all in the game.

Ellery and Nigel Ashley Jones took us pre-season training to Ainsdale beach. It's the worst beach I have ever seen. The tide was out and the water seemed to be about 10 miles away. It was cold and frosty. They had us running on the sand dunes. They had a track going up, down and round the dunes. The sand was soft and giving, we sank in a bit when running and it was really hard on our legs. It was really windy, and cold as the wind comes off the sea. Nigel has all the proper qualifications though, so I'm sure the training benefited us.

Sonny Nickle returned to the club that year, some people may think that with him being involved in the deal to bring me to Saints, he might have some bad feeling towards me, but he didn't. He is a nice fellow and he made some money by going to Bradford. Coming back to St Helens he had the best of both worlds.

The season had some drama in it as in July a big bust up occurred with Ellery Hanley on one side and football manager Eric Hughes and the board on the other. It was nothing to do with me, I was not going to become involved and I didn't want to know what the problems were. It was up to the board to resolve matters with Ellery. I know there were board meetings with Ellery. I thought there always seemed to be people falling out at the club at that time. The players were alright though; Ellery always looked out for the players. We were his main priority. He used to say that if any of us had a problem all we had to do was knock on his door. He was true to his word. If he could help the players he would.

We had a leisure day at Blackpool pleasure beach that season and for some reason bypassed the long queue for The Big One rollercoaster. When the ride finished, the people running it said: 'Go again' and around we went again. This was not good news for some players who felt a bit queasy, as they had no option but to go round again. We went round three times without stopping in the end. I wonder what the people in the queue were thinking.

All year, we played well, but the difference was our discipline. We got the little things right and it showed on the field. He was a very strict coach and I think that took us through to the Super League crown.

## 1999 Grand Final: St Helens versus Bradford Bulls.
Old Trafford. 9 October 1999. Won 8-6.

The 1999 Grand Final was another clash with Bradford. We had lost to them in the qualifying semi-final just two weeks earlier 40-4 at Odsal. Chris Smith had a bad night with kicks towards him. We took the mickey out of Smiggy afterwards, saying he had his hands on back to front. That defeat meant we had to beat Castleford to reach Old Trafford.

Ellery was a cool customer who didn't show much emotion. He just went into the Grand Final as if it was a normal game. We didn't do anything different and he stuck by Smiggy who played well on the big night. Bradford played on the play-off victory during the Grand Final build up, with one of their leading players quoted as saying that he would shout the 40-4 scoreline to Saints players during the final and that Saints could be 'comical' at times. Ellery came into the club during the week of the game and showed us these press reports.

All this fired us up. I think they were complacent, after that big victory over us just before the final. It was a very tough game on a rainy night. Our defence that night was typified by Sonny Nickle's chase after Henry Paul in the first half. Paul scored, but it was a tremendous effort by Sonny. He chased him all the way and if Henry had had to go any further, Sonny would have caught him. I came off early in the second half and was replaced by recent signing Sean Hoppe. Coming into the game I had a tendon problem in my thumb. I missed the Tri Nations series after the Grand Final because I needed an operation to strengthen it.

The main difference between a Challenge Cup Final and a Grand Final is that the venues are different. Old Trafford is spectacular and the Grand Final is the pinnacle of the season, but it is a different atmosphere to the Challenge Cup. The evening kick off at Old Trafford is different as well. But the game of rugby is just the same no matter where it is played. It's the surroundings and settings that affect the atmosphere. It's still a final so it's tense, hard and tight. It was certainly hard for me to watch most of the second half on the bench. I was sitting there and couldn't affect the outcome. I might as well have been a million miles away. I felt like any other spectator.

Kevin Iro's late try and Sean Long's touchline conversion gave us a great win. It was our defence that got us through. The two clubs had a recent history with the two Wembley finals. The Bradford players' motivation was: 'We owe this lot for the two Wembley games'. After the hooter went, Ellery came onto the pitch and spoke to the players. He gave me a hug. He doesn't really show his emotions much, for him to pat someone on the back was a big event. Praise from Ellery really meant something to me.

I found it difficult to get used to the play-off format. Every season I would be asking: 'Who do we play?' 'How does it work again?' 'Are we at home?' 'Have we won it yet?' I could never get to grips with it. Whatever Australia do, we seem to do a season or two later. However, I think it works, it means the title is decided in the last game.

*St Helens:* Atcheson, Smith, Iro, Newlove, Sullivan, Sculthorpe, Martyn, Perelini, Cunningham, O'Neill, Tuilagi, Nickle, Joynt.
Subs: Long, Matautia, Hoppe, Wellens.
*Scorers:* Try: Iro. Goals: Long 2.
*Bradford:* Spruce, Vaikona, Naylor, Withers, Pryce, H. Paul, R. Paul, Anderson, Lowes, Fielden, Boyle, Dwyer, McNamara.
Subs: McAvoy, McDermott, Forshaw, Deacon.
*Scorers:* Try: H. Paul. Goal: H. Paul.

I was picked in the players select XIII that year. To be recognized by my fellow professionals meant I must have been doing something right. It's one of the highest honours a player can get. It was nice to be appreciated by my fellow players at the club too. Being able to get on with people helps lift the morale around a club. From the day I started at the club to the day I left Saints, usually all the players got on with each other. There was no bitching or anything.

Scoring in the corner for St Helens. Chris Joynt and Anthony Sullivan
are watching me touch down. (Photo: Bernard Platt)

Celebrating another St Helens success with our young fans
(Photo: Bernard Platt)

# 8. Morphine daze

The first game of the 2000 season was the resurrected World Club Challenge game against Australian champions Melbourne Storm at the JJB Stadium. We got stuffed 44-6. I don't think Ellery took it seriously to be honest. We never even trained specifically for the game. It was not like the other finals I have been in. We didn't have our strongest side out; Kieron Cunningham wasn't playing for a start. We lost players early on in the game through injury, ended up a bit depleted and it was a long night. It's one of those games best not to remember; a disappointment.

Six weeks later, on 13 March, Ian Millward replaced Ellery as coach at the club. None of the players knew much about him. I didn't know anything about him except that he had come from Leigh and had taken them from the bottom of their Northern Ford Premiership division to the top. This little ginger fellow introduced himself to us in the restaurant. He had his own ideas about the game. I think that every coach should have their own ideas and stick by them and Ian did that. He had us playing a different pattern to what we had been used to with Ellery. We had to adjust to his way of playing and did that pretty quickly.

Before Ian arrived, Leeds had knocked us out of the Challenge Cup. But we must have adapted to Ian's ideas quickly as we won the Super League crown again that year, beating Wigan 29-16 in the Grand Final.

The most memorable event on the pitch in 2000 was Chris Joynt's last second try against Bradford in the play-offs that won us the game. I played my part in creating that try by getting subbed. I cut my head and was on the touchline. The Saints physio Jeannette Smith ran on and I was swapped with Dwayne West in a blood bin substitution.

Time was up, and we were 11-10 down. We had the ball, all the Bradford players were expecting Longy to kick deep so they started to drop back, instead he kicked out wide and their defensive line was shaped like a dog's hind leg. Westy made a break, Joynty supported him, took the pass and touched down. That was it, we had won. It was unbelievable. Longy took St Bernard the mascot's head off and ran back with it on his own head. That's not as bad as what he once did to Bernard. He had scored a try and Bernard came up to cuddle him only to be punched on the nose.

The Grand Final qualifier match was away at Wigan, who had beaten us in the last league game of the season 40-4 at Knowsley Road. I was taken off in the first half with a knee injury, but the side went onto batter Wigan 54-16. Sully scored an amazing try. They put a big up-and-under to him, he caught it and outpaced everyone, turning Gary Connolly inside out in the process.

I missed the Grand Final against Wigan through illness. I had a mouth and throat infection. The week of the final I felt as if I was coming down with flu. I had a blocked nose and was aching all over. I told Jeannette on the Monday that I couldn't train. I came in on Tuesday and told the club that I didn't feel well. They told me to go home and see how I felt later in the week. On Thursday the infection had really taken hold of me. I went to my doctor and he said I would be struggling to play on the Saturday.

He put me on Complan because I hadn't eaten anything as my throat was sore. I had the infection for a long time. I lost about a stone through it. I was starving, but couldn't eat as every time I swallowed, it was like swallowing glass. I was pale, had ulcers and was in a right mess. There was no way I could have played. I might have dropped down dead if I had played, I was that weak. I wasn't going to go to the game as I didn't feel right. Joynty and Ian Millward both rang me up though and told me to come, saying that the lads wanted me to come. I went across and watched the game. I was thrilled for everybody that we won and for myself as I had played all year. I got my Super League ring and had played my part through the season.

Under Ian's coaching, we went on to become World Club champions in 2001; beating Brisbane Broncos 20-18 at the Reebok Stadium in Bolton after we had been 12-6 down at half time. We also lifted the Challenge Cup, beating Bradford 13-6 at Twickenham.

## 2001 World Club Challenge: St Helens versus Brisbane Broncos.
Reebok Stadium, Bolton. 26 January 2001. Won 20-18.

This match was my 400th career appearance. We looked at their team which included Darren Lockyer, Wendell Sailor, Lote Tuqiri, Shane Webcke and Gorden Tallis and it was a daunting prospect. Playing any top Australian side is tough as everyone builds them up so much that we think they are better than us. At the end of the day, they're not. We went to Lanzarote before the Brisbane game, that week was really important. We could see that Ian Millward wanted a big week out of us and he got it. We were really switched on and it helped us build up for the game. The training sessions were good and everybody was focused. The players were up for the game, which was taking place at the Reebok Stadium, Bolton, rather than Knowsley Road.

Early on, I gave my opposite number Stuart Kelly the outside and dragged him into touch. It wasn't a copybook tackle, but it was effective. I did a couple of tackles on Gorden Tallis early on; a few of us were trying to get him down. It was the same with Wendell Sailor. When those two came onto the ball we had to get up to them really quickly before they got into their stride. Then we just hoped for the best. If we could hang on to them, the other players could help. I have played against Sailor a few times and he is always talking, things like 'what's the score?' and 'how much money are you on?' He was trying to put me off my game. Other players have tried it, but I don't get drawn into all that.

People said that as my career developed my defence improved and I would agree. I recently watched a video of me playing for Great Britain against France when I was young and my defence was shocking. When I arrived at Saints, I thought my defence improved as I got older. I felt my positional play got better as well. I think Ian Millward had a lot to do with that. He used to tell me to keep my feet moving. It all comes together, I was never a copybook - round the legs - style of tackler but I could clamp the ball. Nobody would usually get round me.

Brisbane were very confident when they went 12-6 and later 18-6 up against us. To come back from 18-6 down against the best team in the world took some doing. It was a big achievement and took a big effort. We all played well. The cold and the hailstones that hammered down also helped. I don't think Brisbane had ever experienced anything like that before. Sean Long had just gone in for a try to make it 18-12 and their players were standing behind the posts. I don't know if they were shaking with the cold, but their heads were a bit down and they must have thought: 'What are we in here?' All our lads were buzzing then, including Dave Fairleigh who was making his debut that night. He was shouting out orders and encouragement. He was up for it and had a big game, as did Peter Shiels. They had experience of playing against Brisbane through their careers in Australia and knew how tough it was going to be. In team meetings they told us about the Broncos which was very helpful.

There was a key moment in the game. I got the ball on the left and Sailor came up a bit too quickly. I came off my left, then stepped back out and was clear then. I had Sully on my left and Joynty inside me. Joynty has scored a lot of tries like that when I've broken through. I had two options. Lockyer didn't come at me straight away. He was trying to weigh me up to see what I was going to do. He came at me and I had made my mind up pretty early to give the ball to Joynty because I was running that angle. Sully didn't have much room to play with and if I had passed to him I think Lockyer would have taken him. My best option was Joynty and when the time was right I drew Lockyer and Joynty scored. As Joynty went in, Tallis came in to him late. I thought it was going to start a fight. Tallis jumped up, there was a bit of pushing and shoving and a few words exchanged, but there was no proper fighting. I thought: 'You don't want to be fighting with Gorden, Chris'. That try and the subsequent conversion made the score 18-18.

I took a kick from Lockyer really low down near our line which earned me some praise from Sky commentator Phil Clarke. It was a difficult ball to take, but if I had knocked on, it would have been their scrum and another set of six for them on our line. Fortunately, I took it. Our concentration levels at that time were really high. I didn't have time to think, a click of the fingers and the moment's gone, that's how switched on we were. Scully and Longy popped drop goals over to give us the winning lead. A one pointer is as good as two points sometimes when it's near the end of the game. As the hooter approaches in a tight game, to come away from their end of the field with something is great. We kept chipping away at them.

Sky's Eddie Hemmings said that it was one of the best games of my life. It was similar to a Grand Final, maybe even better. To beat Brisbane was such an achievement. I have my shirt from that game framed and on the wall in a room in my house. It's a superb feeling being a world champion. I went to the crowd after the hooter and was really giving it out. I was going barmy, Sky captured me shouting at the crowd and holding the Saints badge on my shirt as players sometimes do. I just thought that everybody played really well. The crowd was tremendous, all our speccies were there, the neutrals wanted us to win, well apart from the

Wigan fans shouting for Brisbane. I was emotional and excited with the win.

Australian sides are used to playing in touch-and-go games. One sided games in the Australian competition are fairly rare, and are more common in Britain. It's important to be used to an arm wrestle type of game and the Australians are used to those games. We were the first British team to win the resurrected World Club Challenge and it was a shot in the arm for British Rugby League. Since our win, Bradford have won the game twice. I know the Australians come over here. If it was the other way round, would we compete? I don't know as it's a long way and a big ask as I think the players need a few weeks to acclimatise.

*St Helens:* Wellens, Hoppe, Iro, Newlove, Sullivan, Martyn, Long, Fairleigh, Cunningham, Nickle, Joynt, Shiels, Sculthorpe.
Subs: Stewart, Matautia, Jonkers, Stankevitch.
*Scorers:* Tries: Long, Sculthorpe, Joynt. Goals: Long 3. Drop Goals: Long, Sculthorpe.
*Brisbane:* Lockyer; Sailor, Kelly, De Vere, Tuqiri; Berrigan, Prince, Webcke, Priddis, Civoniceva; Tallis, Carlaw; Lee.
Subs: Meyers, C. Walker, S. Walker, Harrison.
*Scorers:* Tries: Berrigan, Lee, Meyers. Goals: De Vere 3.

I felt that we were now a step ahead of everybody. Previously the shout was 'get deep' and run onto the ball. Ian changed that to a flatter style of attack. It worked for us. No matter who the coach is; Saints' sides always play with flair. They have always been a team to throw the ball about, people say Saints can't defend, but Saints usually score more points than the opposition.

Having said that, I think the old 'Saints can't defend' line isn't strictly true. I've played in Saints games where we defended really well. The tag of 'The Entertainers' suits Saints; they are a side who will try passes even in their own 25. Ian even said: 'What's the difference between passing the ball in their 25 and your own 25? No matter where you are on the field, if the pass is on, it's still the same pass you are making'. We attacked from deep, had the pace out wide and got results. I don't think the Saints' style of play will change in the future. Attack is what the supporters expect.

In 2001, Saints beat Wigan in the Challenge Cup, and were drawn away to Whitehaven. The changing rooms there were tiny. We stopped at a hotel just outside Whitehaven, got changed there, strapped and rubbed down and jumped on the bus. We had two or three minutes in the changing room then went out to play. It's a long journey there as well.

We went onto the Challenge Cup Final, beating Huddersfield and Leeds after our trip to Cumbria. But the week before the Twickenham Final I was sent off at Warrington. I was thinking surely the disciplinary committee wouldn't ban me from the Final. My disciplinary record was excellent and the sending off wasn't for a malicious tackle. There was no intent, Toa Kohe-Love had wrong footed me and I had put my arm up. Toa got up straight away, he wasn't hurt and I think the referee made too much out of it. Having said that, at the back of my mind was the thought that it might not turn out right and I would miss the Final. I went to Leeds for the hearing. It was a new experience for me, all this procedure - it was like being in court. Phil Clarke's dad Colin was on the committee along with Wilf George, who I had played against. They had a judge there who was the main man on the top table. They asked: 'Do you have anything to say Mr Newlove?' I didn't miss the Final, and was glad to get the hearing over. I was really nervous.

**2001 Challenge Cup Final: St Helens versus Bradford Bulls.**
Twickenham. 28 April 2001. Won 13-6.

Before the Final, Saints took us down to Twickenham to watch England play Italy there as they wanted us to experience what the ground was like when it was full. This was so that when we played there on the day we would know what it was like. We were booked into an excellent hotel in the middle of London. We had tickets for the game and were sitting very high up. It's a tremendous stadium; as for the game England were winning very easily early on. Even with the lowly opposition of Italy, Twickenham was full. Near the end, we said: 'Let's get out of here' and went to a pub outside the ground.

It was an experience playing at Twickenham, with that and later Murrayfield the only major British rugby union stadium I didn't play at was the Millennium Stadium in Cardiff. Twickenham had massive changing rooms. There was an enormous crowd there; it was really special.

During the week of the game, we had a filmed training session with comedian Johnny Vegas, who is from St Helens and a big Saints supporter. They made out on television that Johnny was going to play for Saints and Ian Millward was giving him a trial. Ian put Johnny into training and introduced him to us all. It was all set up. We had to do a drill and Johnny was holding the pads. They got Vila Matautia to run at him, Vila gave him everything and sent him flying. To be fair, Johnny had told him: 'Don't hold back'. He wanted him to run into him to make it look real. Vila certainly didn't let him down. We were all shouting: 'Go on, Vila'. He just ran over the top of him. Johnny then pulled out a Mars Bar out of his sock and started eating it. It was always funny around him.

He has done a lot for Saints. He wears club merchandise when he is on programmes such as *Shooting Stars* and mentioned the club when he won best newcomer at the Comedy Awards a few years back.

Tony Blair was guest of honour at Twickenham so I was introduced to him. It would have been nice for the Queen to have presented the cup one year, but it never happened in one of my cup finals.

The first half was pretty warm, then in the second half it started to rain. It lashed down. In the first half, I cracked Joe Vagana with a high tackle. He didn't know who had hit him and thought it was Chris Joynt so he gave Joynty a dig while I walked away unscathed. Joynty took the brunt once again. I think that's why he has lost his hair on top, it's from people punching him or rubbing his head on top. The second half was very tight, we went in at half time 13-4 up. The full time score was 13-6. We didn't concede a try. Sean Long put a kick through in the first half for Tommy Martyn to score. He did it again for Keiron Cunningham to score our second try. Bradford didn't look like scoring a try as our defence was brilliant. Henry Paul scored all their points from penalties.

The first half was full on. There was one tackle where I caught Henry Paul just right and Tommy Martyn gave me a big pat on the back. I liked having Tommy inside me, he was a great defender. He also had pace and I had great confidence with him there. Our left hand side defence was strong: Joynty, Tommy, Sully and me. We were a really solid unit. At Saints, in training, we used to work in these little units. There was competition between the left and right hand sides. We did left versus right in training with one side defending and the other attacking. In a game we would say: 'No tries down this side'. If the opposition scored on the right we would say: 'They didn't score down our side'. It was our job to protect our side. If all the tries were scored on the right or down the middle, we'd done our job. Of course, we would always try to come across and help out. There's more to organising the defence than people realise, and we were solid that day.

We watched the video in the dressing room at half time. We were the only club doing that then. Ian Millward had a laptop and at half time he would connect the laptop to the television. He could show us a breakdown of the first half, anything that had happened during the game he wanted to change. Before a game, the system was also useful, and provided information on the opposition. After the game, everything we did in the game would be transferred onto the laptop so through the week each player could go to Ian and look at their performance. He would give you feedback on your good and bad points that week. The software costs a lot of money, but it gave us an edge over other teams.

I got taken off 10 minutes into the second half with a pulled hamstring. I don't know where it came from as I was fine in the first half. Maybe it was the wet conditions, but I got a little twinge in it and couldn't carry on. I had to sit it out. Our physio put a blanket on me as it was cold, dark and rainy for the rest of the game. The last 20 minutes were hard to watch. I always seemed to be injured during finals, that or I missed them through illness.

Sean Long's kicking game was excellent that day. The grass was very long on the pitch, the same as at Murrayfield. Rugby union must prefer long grass, because rugby league pitches usually have short grass. It wasn't the best playing surface for us.

We were the first side to complete the treble of winning the Super League trophy, the Challenge Cup and the World Club Challenge. The photos from that day show us sticking three fingers up. It was a great achievement.

*Bradford Bulls:* Withers, Vaikona, Naylor, Rigon, Pryce, H. Paul, R. Paul, Vagana, Lowes, McDermott, Peacock, Gartner, Forshaw.
Subs: Deacon, Anderson, Fielden, Gilmour.
*Scorers:* Goals: H. Paul 3.
*St Helens:* Wellens, Hoppe, Iro, Newlove, Sullivan, Martyn, Long, Fairleigh, Cunningham, Nickle, Joynt, Shiels, Sculthorpe.
Subs: Hall, Stewart, Matautia, Jonkers.
*Scorers:* Tries: Martyn, Cunningham. Goals: Long 2. Drop Goal: Martyn.

On 2 July 2001 we played Hull away and went down to a 34-28 defeat. I scored, but the big event for me was an Achilles injury which put me out for the rest of the season. I had been playing well and was Saints' top try scorer. My Achilles tendons were sore until I had warmed up. I was told to make sure I got a good rub on them to get them warm. I did that, but the soreness was still there. I carried on playing and then came the Hull game. Early on I took an interception, went nearly the full length of the field and scored. I thought then that if my Achilles was going to be a problem, it would have shown up while I was running all that way. I thought I'm warmed up now and I'll be fine.

The game went on, about 10 minutes before half time I got the ball, stepped, went through a gap and there was a sound like a twig snapping.

Chris Smith was playing for Hull that day. Smiggy is a good mate of mine, but I thought he had kicked me on the back of my leg. I went down, everyone around heard it snap. It was really aching. They took me off and we knew straight away that my Achilles had gone. Claire Mannion was the new Saints physio and she did a test where the player kneels up on a bench in the dressing room, they squeeze the player's calf and their heel should move. They did this test and my heel didn't move.

After half time I was left in the dressing room alone with an ice pack on my Achilles. I had not taken any painkillers and it really hurt. Saints' dressing room assistant Billy Bates came in to see how I was and I asked him to go get the doctor to give me some painkillers. I got some, but they didn't make any difference. I lay on the dressing room bench for the whole of the second half. After that, Claire strapped me up. Adele's mum and dad took me home in their car. Two days after that I was in the hospital at Oswestry and had an operation. They took the tendons from my hamstring, plaited them together to make them really strong and then sewed it all into the gap. It's better than my other one now, so to truly confuse people I say my bad one is now my good one and my good one is now my bad one. Work it out.

I remember the date of the operation because the tennis at Wimbledon was on and it was very hot. Now, whenever Wimbledon comes round it reminds me of my Achilles snapping. All I did while I was laid up was watch Wimbledon. I remember being in the hospital bed in my own room. My foot was in a pot and I had to sleep with it elevated. The hospital beds have plastic covers on them in case any patients wet themselves. That was sticking to me because the plastic sheet makes you sweat. My foot was aching all night and I was on morphine. The nurse told me that whenever I felt pain I should click the button and it would give me another shot of morphine. They took it away from me in the end because I used it all up. Every 10 minutes, I clicked it and boom, I was down again. It was great. I don't know how much I used, but they disconnected it. That morphine was wonderful, I was so 'morphined up' I couldn't even lift my arms. I went to use the telephone, no doubt grinning like a Cheshire cat. I couldn't move and promptly went back to sleep.

After a while, the pain came back so the nurse returned with a pill that had to be taken - how shall I put this - up my rear end. I had to bend over, she shoved it up, whoa, chuffing hell, I didn't like that. It took my mind off my foot. I was in the hospital for three days, they wanted to keep me in longer, but also wanted my bed so I would have had to move to the main ward.

I didn't fancy that as I had my own telly in my room, so said if I left the room I was going home. Before they let me go home though, they wanted to see me go to the toilet. I came out of the anaesthetic after the operation and didn't urinate for three days. I'm not sure if it was the morphine affecting me. This nurse took me to the toilet, she was stood behind me, not watching me, but made me go to the toilet. In the end I managed it. The problem was standing up after lying in bed for three days; I could feel the blood rush down to my foot. It felt awful. It was nine months until I returned to playing.

The rehab was really boring. I couldn't do much, but what I did do was very repetitive. I asked if we could vary it or do something different, but I had to do what I was told. I had to grit my teeth and get on with it. It included kicking my legs in the swimming pool, trying to get my Achilles working again as fast as possible. I take my hat off to Claire, she did really well. I know I was maybe a bit of a pain for her, but I'd never experienced rehab before.

Training on my own was a new experience as well. Obviously, throughout any career players get injuries and might miss a week or two, but recovering from a long term injury is tough. I missed the company of the other players. I was alone in the gym doing step-ups and calf-raises to get my muscles back working. Joynty did a few sessions with me in the morning which was helpful. We used to go to a David Lloyd club for swimming and it was nice having someone else to talk to. It all helped.

Saints asked me if I would see a psychiatrist. I am positive I hadn't started talking to myself so don't know whose idea that was; it might have been Ian Millward's. I was quite happy just to do my rehab. Anyway they got this guy in called Darren Robinson, a sports psychologist. He was doing some work for Derby County at the time. They put him onto me, they told me that nobody would know and that he would see me at the David Lloyd club and I could sit down and talk to him. He was goal-setting for me and everything. What he also did was train with me, he used to do weights with me which was supportive.

He was good to talk to though. Ian Millward would be asking: 'How are you going?' because Claire had me running on the field. When they saw me running, they were saying 'he is running well, he looks alright'. What they saw and how I felt I was running were two completely different things. Ian Millward kept on saying that he was thinking about playing me soon and I kept telling him I wasn't ready. I thought he was interfering a bit, but it was understandable as he wanted me back. It was good to talk to Darren because he wasn't concerned about getting me back into the side. For a long time, I wasn't sure about making the step to play again.

Ian Millward pencilled me in for the beginning of Super League in 2002, away at Widnes on 2 March. There was no chance of me playing friendlies or the first two Challenge Cup matches, so I was going into the season without any match fitness which I didn't like. He kept saying to me that Widnes was the aim for me. I didn't think I was ready. So it was put back to the home game against Salford the next week and again I didn't feel that I wanted to play. I couldn't run properly, I was hobbling. Funnily enough I scored against Salford. I don't know how I managed it. I threw a big dummy and they took it. We won 34-2, and I didn't play the full game. When I came off the field I was relieved and felt I had regained some confidence.

After that game, in each match Ian would play me for half an hour then bring me off. Then he might play me for 40 minutes and bring me off. He did this to gradually bring me back into it. After a few games he asked me how I was feeling and said that if I had any twinges I should come off, no questions asked.

Ask anyone who has had a knee reconstruction, players such as Tommy Martyn and Sean Long and they'll say that the first game back after a big operation is hard psychologically.

For pre-season training the team went to Marbella. I did my shuttle runs and hopping. It was rehab work separate from the rest of the team as I couldn't do full contact. Sonny Nickle was injured at the time as well, so he trained with me. Kel Coslett was team manager and he monitored our progress. I'm sure he would confirm how hard I worked then. I had to get my balance back. I also had to build up the muscle on my calf, it had really deteriorated. It's still not as big as my other one to this day. Eventually I got back to playing rugby.

Everyone had been saying that I was finished and would retire. They all wrote me off and I proved them wrong. I am actually the quickest sportsman to come back from this type of Achilles injury. Claire even had football clubs ringing her up to enquire about the rehab work I had done.

The warm weather training camps out of the country each January were great. They were hard work, we trained three or four times a day. We had the sun on our backs and could get more done. We weren't trying to catch the ball in the hail and snow with numb fingers.

I used to hate Christmas and New Year as in the winter rugby era there were games on Boxing Day and New Year's Day so the players couldn't join in with everybody else's celebrations. When summer rugby came round I thought: 'Well, at least I'll get my Christmas and New Year back'. How wrong I was. The clubs started playing friendlies over the holiday period. Saints had a game against Wigan on Boxing Day. It was a money-making exercise as I suppose it was a long time to go without gate receipts coming in between seasons.

Ian Millward was good about those matches when he took over at Saints. He would ask me which one I wanted to play in. I would always choose the Boxing Day game rather than New Year's Day. There's usually a big party on New Year's Eve, and I would want to be involved in that. One Boxing Day we played and Saints fielded me alongside a team full of kids. Ian Millward took me off for the last 15 minutes.

It was frustrating when I couldn't fully take part on Christmas Day when everybody else was getting stuck into food and drink. Players still have to watch what they eat and can't let themselves go and have an extra pudding. For me those days have gone now, thankfully and I can enjoy Christmas with my family.

The highlight of 2002 was the Super League Grand Final. It made up for the disappointment of losing in the Challenge Cup Final at Murrayfield to Wigan.

## 2002 Challenge Cup Final:
## St Helens versus Wigan Warriors.
Murrayfield. 27 April 2002. Lost 21-12.

I think we were complacent in the lead up to Murrayfield. We trained on a little rugby union field before the Final and the session was poor. There were dropped balls everywhere, no coordination and no communication. It was very low key for a Final; poor. We had beaten Wigan 19-0 four weeks before the Final and I think they played on the underdogs tag. They said that Radlinski wouldn't be playing and they had so many injuries. They tried to pull the wool over our eyes and maybe we fell for it, although to be fair Radlinski did have a nasty injury.

We read in the press that it was going to be a one sided Final for Saints. But on the day we were useless. However, I was voted Saints players' player-of-the-match back at the hotel. I thought I had had a really good first half. Every time I got the ball, I seemed to be making a break and also came close to scoring. But in the second half, the team just didn't use me. I think I only got two passes in the second half, it just went dead.

It just wasn't meant to be. I think rugby league is all on the day. A bounce of the ball, a referee's decision, it's all on the day. It is how the players wake up in a morning, I'm sure it is. I know we prepare, but it's also if it's meant to be, it's meant to be. It was hard losing the Cup Final. Playing up at Murrayfield didn't impress me, it took an edge off it. There was a small stand on one side whereas Twickenham was like the Coliseum. We can't blame that, I'm not making excuses for us losing.

I've always said I would rather lose in the rounds before the final than in the final itself. There's nothing for you in losing a final, I know people say: 'At least you got there' but I'd rather lose in the first round.

*St Helens:* Wellens, Stewart, Newlove, Gleeson, Albert, Martyn, Long, Britt, Cunningham, Shiels, Joynt, Jonkers, Sculthorpe.
Subs: Higham, Stankevitch, Hoppe, Ward.
*Scorers:* Tries: Albert, Gleeson, Sculthorpe.
*Wigan Warriors:* Radlinski, Johnson, Connolly, Ainscough, Dallas, O'Neill, Lam, O'Connor, Newton, C. Smith, Cassidy, Furner, Farrell.
Subs: Carney, Hodgson, M. Smith, Bibey.
*Scorers:* Tries: Dallas, Lam, Connolly. Goals: Farrell 4. Drop goal: Lam.

## 2002 Grand Final: St Helens versus Bradford Bulls.
Old Trafford. 19 October 2002. Won 19-18.

After Murrayfield, there was only the Grand Final to play for. Losing a Challenge Cup Final is awful, it ruins the whole weekend. We knew we had to go back to St Helens and the turn out when we got back was poor. Once it's done, it's done though. The week after, we were back into training, and had to forget about it and soldier on. It is a factor in the Grand Final though. We said in our team talks: 'Remember how we felt when we lost the final and we don't want to feel like that again'. It kicked us on. If we had won the Challenge Cup it might have made us complacent and we might not have won the Grand Final, who knows?

I had a bit of a groin pull leading up to the game. I was taken off the previous week when we knocked Wigan out of the play-offs on a wet night at Knowsley Road. I made a break, fell on my knees and then did the splits because the surface was so wet.

The Grand Final came closer. I trained towards the end of the week and knew I would be alright to play. I thought we didn't play that well, especially in the first 30 minutes or so. As the game went on, we became a bit more composed.

Paul Wellens was in a bad way after fracturing his cheekbone in the opening minutes. When we came in to the changing room after the game, everybody was so high with our victory, singing and chanting while poor Wello was sitting there with his face swollen. He looked a right mess. I don't know what he was feeling, but I'm sure he must have been pleased for the team.

Bradford scored as soon as Paul was injured, so we were 6-0 down, with no full back on the field, after just a couple of minutes. They started better than we did and threw everything at us in the first 20 minutes. They also had a Paul Deacon try disallowed by the video referee. I was involved in the incident. I was falling backwards trying to collect the ball as Jamie Peacock was after it. The video referee felt that Peacock had reefed the ball from me. I thought it was touch-and-go. If they had scored then, we would have been 12-0 down and in a bit of trouble. We got by it though and somehow went in at the break 12-8 in front.

Bradford fought back for an 18-12 lead, but then Martin Gleeson touched down out wide. Eight minutes later, Sean Long made the score 18-18 with a penalty in front of the posts. After Gleeson's try,

Paul Sculthorpe gathered the team together to talk to us. He encouraged us to step up a gear.

The last quarter of the game remains vividly in my mind as both sides went at it toe-to-toe. We knew that the team that made the next mistake would lose. We just played our sets of six, Ian had always told us: 'Don't panic, just play your sets of six, play your normal game'. Bradford were kicking long, turning our full back and wingers round. Coming out of our half, the back three did exceptionally well. They had brought the ball back well all year. The back three at Saints is still strong because Ian tells them to pass to each other. That created the match-winning opportunity. The score was 18-18 with only a minute left. Sean Hoppe had collected the ball and passed it to Darren Albert, he took it on further. Tony Stewart came off his wing and made a break. I took it in, making headway towards the middle. There was no call for a drop goal; we just knew what had to be done. Players are not precisely aware of how long is left in a game. We don't have time to look at the clock on the big screen. When there's a break in play or a penalty we might have a look then to find out how long is left. All we knew was that time was nearly up. Longy put the drop goal over and that made it 19-18.

I think because we had been in so many big games and had to come from behind to win some of them helped us. When Wigan dominated the game, they were the same and always had the ability to compose themselves at key moments. We were the same at St Helens. We refused to panic. It's easier said than done, but it is essential to play how you train to play no matter what the occasion or situation. We came away with something most of the time. It went for us on this occasion. I'm sure our big match experience played on the minds of our opponents too and they thought 'Saints are going to do it again. Saints can come back at any time.' While the game is alive, Saints aren't finished. The opposition were aware of that.

It was another tense game and extra time had been a real possibility. It didn't cross my mind at the time although it had done prior to the game as the match programme said there would be extra time if the scores were level after 80 minutes.

I was delighted when Longy's drop goal went over. We had been under pressure and had had to play error-free rugby to have a chance. We knew that the next dropped ball would be punished. The drop goal wasn't quite the end of the drama, there was the controversial Chris Joynt 'voluntary tackle', when he went down with the ball in the closing seconds. I don't think it was a voluntary tackle, in my opinion he was tricked into doing it. As I saw it, Chris was preparing himself to be tackled and I thought Deacon got out of the way. Chris fell onto the floor waiting for the collision, then got back up straight away. He didn't flounder or anything. It was a talking point for sure and Bradford were adamant it should have been a penalty, which if converted would have given them the match. We were too busy jumping about congratulating each other to see some Bradford players protest after the final hooter. What's the referee going to do? He can't change the result; he can't say 'alright I'll give the penalty now'. It was just understandable frustration.

As we all sang 'Oh when the Saints' on the podium with the Super League trophy as fireworks went off overhead, I didn't think that this would be my last final. I thought I would have got another one in, either a Challenge Cup Final or a Grand Final.

It was another superb moment on that podium though. All those moments are different but all merge together. It's hard to explain, everyone is so happy. Champagne is flying about, 'We are the champions' is booming out around the stadium. The noise of the crowd is amazing. There's no better feeling; well, maybe winning the lottery. I will always remember bringing the trophy round to thousands of our supporters. Everyone is cheering and waving flags and banners. I always liked reading the banners, some were really witty.

All five domestic finals that I won were against the Bulls. It must hurt them. Every final, people were saying Saints' hoodoo over Bradford had to end, but it didn't. We kept them at bay and performed better than them.

This was our fourth league title in seven years and if I knew the secret to Saints' success, I would be the coach of one of the big clubs. The blend of the side was crucial. We had flair, could defend and went right to the end of matches. Every team has three or four players the opposition have to beware of, but I think Saints had more than that. A consistent line-up is important and Saints manage to do that. I won eight trophies during my time at the club. I went to Saints for trophies and to get success in the game. I made the right choice in joining the club.

*St Helens:* Wellens, Stewart, Gleeson, Newlove, Albert, Sculthorpe, Long, Britt, Cunningham, Ward, Jonkers, Bennett, Joynt.
Subs: Stankevitch, Higham, Shiels, Hoppe.
*Scorers:* Tries: Bennett, Long, Gleeson. Goals: Long 3. Drop Goal: Long.
*Bradford:* Withers; Vaikona, Naylor, Costin, Vainikolo; Paul, Deacon, Vagana, Lowes, Fielden, Gartner, Peacock, Forshaw.
Subs: Pryce, McDermott, Anderson, Gilmour.
*Scorers:* Tries: Naylor, Paul, Withers. Goals: Deacon 3.

## Claire Mannion is the St Helens physio and helped Paul recover from his serious Achilles injury in 2001.

"When Paul did his Achilles, Kevin Iro told him to get on the bench so he could have a look as Kevin had suffered the same injury in the past. Kevin and I had a look at him and told him that it was an Achilles injury and was very serious. Paul just said: 'You think you're so funny', but we had to tell him we weren't joking.

When Paul had his Achilles operation, they took his hamstring tendons and reconstructed his Achilles by plaiting those tendons into the Achilles, as he had a complete rupture. After the operation he said to me: 'I'm not going to make it back from this am I?' and I told him: 'With that attitude, no, you're not'. He was very difficult to rehab as he had never had an injury before that would keep him out for a long period. He did hit rock bottom on several occasions and was quite difficult to work with as he, I am sure, would be the first to admit. There were a lot of lows as well as a lot of highs.

I know he has said he was a bit of a pain, he was more than that. After the operation, the hospital sent Paul home with really strong painkillers. He came out of the hospital on the Friday and he rang me on the Monday to say: 'I need some more of those painkillers'. It turned out he had taken two weeks supply. I told him he could have killed himself and he replied: 'I'm still talking aren't I?'

We went pre-season training in Marbella and that week was the longest of my life. He didn't want to do anything. In the past all he had to do was lie back, think of England and his injuries healed. This time, he had to put some effort in and do the work. It was only he who could get himself back on the pitch with a bit of guidance. He just couldn't get his head round that.

To be fair, it was a horrific injury, he couldn't walk. It took him three months to walk properly. When he did get back to walking, it was really hard. Then to get him from walking to jogging was a mammoth task. He did exceptionally well. I thought that it was he who was going to hold him back rather than the injury itself. It was going to take a lot of guts and determination from him and me to get him back playing because I was determined that he wasn't going to give in.

As I said, Paul didn't want to do any extra training in Marbella. One idea was to put me and him in a rowing boat. I said: 'There is no way I am getting in a boat with him. I don't like water and I know he's not going to do any rowing'.

He's an introverted person until people get to know him. I had the opportunity to get to know him and he's completely different to the personality he often portrays. He's very sharp-witted and charismatic, but keeps himself to himself, and plays his cards very close to his chest. He doesn't have a big interest in sport when he's not playing. I remember Saints playing Wigan in the 2001 play-off eliminator while he was out injured. He rang me after the game saying: 'Come on then, did we beat them?' He wasn't going to see half that Saints team again as a few of them were leaving the club.

I remember at Twickenham when we had won the Challenge Cup Final. All the players boarded the team bus with their kit in sport bags, Paul came walking onto the bus with his kit in a black bin liner. I always remember Eric Ashton saying: 'Newy, you look like a rat catcher'.

Paul watched *Emmerdale* week in, week out and there was a time when we were all gathered round for a meeting when Saints were in London. Paul blurted out: 'Come on, hurry up with this meeting'. We asked why and he said: 'Because tonight we find out what happens to Jack, he could go down for murder tonight'. We asked him what he was on about and he told us it was a story on *Emmerdale*.

Then there was the time he dislocated his thumb. He had it pinned and reconstructed. The first thing he said when he got to the hospital bed was: 'So am I going to get a full English breakfast in the morning?'

There are so many stories about him, such as him and Chris Smith coming into the club and selling Christmas trees. He was just one of the characters of the club and the game, unfortunately not many people get to see that side of his personality.

I remember him turning round in the dressing room one day and saying: 'Rugby would be alright if you didn't have to train'. I said to him: 'That's your job'. He is the laziest person on two feet.

He just wouldn't apply himself. He is also tighter than tight. I remember one of the training camps in Lanzarote and we all went out for a meal and Newy just told a few of us to walk out with him. I pointed out that he hadn't paid the bill and he said: 'If they're too drunk to notice we've gone, let them pay'. He just walked out. I used to go to the David Lloyd club with him and I nearly fell over when he offered to buy me some sandwiches for my dinner.

Having said all that, he is such a great person to be around. People in the game who know him, love him for the way he is.

With Chris Joynt and the Super League Trophy
(Photo: Bernard Platt)

With the Challenge Cup and Super League trophies in 1996
(Photo: Bernard Platt)

A happy moment with St Helens
(Photo: Bernard Platt)

Playing against the Brisbane Broncos in the 2001 World Club Challenge
(Photo: Bernard Platt)

# 9. Great Saints

I played with many great players and characters in my time at Knowsley Road. What follows is a selection of memories and people.

Chris Joynt was one of my closest friends at the club. I always roomed with him if I could when we went away with Saints, at the pre-season training camps or if we were playing in London. It's different when we went away with Great Britain as they might pair me with my wing partner and put the second rows together.

I think Stan Wall did the room list for Saints and he knew who to put together. We all got on with each other, but it was better to put Chris and me together rather than having one of us with one of the young kids. We have similar personalities, although I think Chris is a bit lazier than me. He could sleep on a washing line; as soon as his head touches the pillow he's asleep. He's always snoozing, he's like a big, lazy dog. As for supping tea, he's always after a brew and he was always asking me to make it. We used to argue over whose turn it was. When he was in bed and I was mooching about trying not to make noise or coming in at night he would always wake up and say: 'Make a bit more noise Newy, I can't hear you'. A typical comment from him, but we had some laughs together.

I lent him my dog Jack. He's still got it. I had just bought my current house, it was a little bungalow when I got it and I wanted to extend it. I got planning permission and got the builders in. It was meant to be three months work, but it went on a bit longer than that. We had to move into a flat with Adele's sister. There was no room for the dog, and he would have had to go into kennels. Previously I had put him in kennels and he had a stroke as he was upset there. Some pets are like that when they're taken away from home. I knew I couldn't take him back to the kennels and Joynty said he would look after him while the work was being done. I just had to pay for the dog's food. Every so often Joynty would say to me: 'We're a bit low on Pedigree Chum, Newy'. I would turn up with a crate of 24 tins, not beers but dog food. I threw in some chews for him as well. 'Chews?' Joynty said, 'He's chewed all my doors'.

He is a Staffordshire Bull Terrier, he is friendly, but big and strong. He would jump up at the doors to see what was happening in the room. He chewed Joynty's rocking chair as well and Joynty ended up palming the dog off on his mum and dad. He did the same to their doors. I used to go round to Joynty's and he lives round the corner from his mum and dad, so we would call in on them. His dad used to say: 'When that bloody dog dies Chris, you are going to pay for every door in this house'. Joynty was going mad, and said to me: 'Bloody hell, Newy, you're costing me a fortune'. When he found out I had a horse he said: 'Don't bring that down here, we're not looking after it'.

I played with Joynty for Great Britain in the home test series against New Zealand in 1998. I can see it now; we were in our own 25. The hooter went for half time, Joe Vagana was at dummy-half and Joynty was at marker. Joynty just turned round and started walking off, the referee said 'play on' as the ball was in motion. Vagana picked up the ball and scored as Joynty was walking off as if he was strolling down the road. I thought: 'What's gone on here?' Maybe he was thinking of his half time brew. I can tell that story now. It's funny now, but it wasn't at the time.

People remember my partnership with Anthony Sullivan and the understanding we had on the field. We never really worked at it. It just happened, he could read me. The only thing I ever said to him was for him to hold his touchline and let me come to him, and not to start cutting inside. I could draw my centre and winger at the same time, then slip a ball to my wingman, it was a move I liked to do. If I could go myself I would, otherwise I would try and put Sully away. He was a great finisher and had great pace. I remember in 1998, we won 37-22 against London Broncos at The Stoop. Sully scored five tries and I set them all up for him.

Kieron Cunningham is tremendous. I remember first seeing him in a televised game in the 1995 Challenge Cup when Saints drew 16-16 with Wigan at Central Park. He was only a kid and he had a belting game. His work rate and effort are incredible, he never stops. He's a chunky fellow and his speed from dummy half and his agility are amazing. He is probably the best hooker in the world, he's got it all.

Apollo Perelini is a nice fellow and a committed Christian. He never tried to push his faith onto me though which is a relief. There are enough bashings in rugby league without being subjected to a Bible bashing. He switched codes and once he learnt about league he was a really good forward. In 1996 he was scoring long range tries, and bagged 12 that year. He was sprinting, pushing people off and side-stepping like a centre. His physique was unbelievable.

I had played against Kevin Iro, but never really knew him until he joined Saints. Carl Hall is a friend of mine and tried to get me to join Leeds when one of my contracts at Saints was due to end. Kevin was pushing me to come there as well as he was at Leeds then. It didn't happen, but later on I was pushing for Kevin to join me a Saints. He is a big man. He didn't throw silly weights round in the gym, just did his own little routine. He was naturally gifted and his ability on the field was unbelievable. He could push anybody off and was quick as well for a big fellow. He could slip balls out and was very dangerous to play against. I'd rather play with him than against him. He's another nice guy and he used to travel with me across the Pennines to St Helens. The toughest players I played against were definitely Kevin Iro and Richie Blackmore. They were my opposite centres who were big and mobile and could defend.

Scott Gibbs was a chunky fellow, good player, strong as a bull with a good pair of hands on him. I think he never really enjoyed rugby league though, and returned to union, although he said in his book that he loved the game. I think he found the greater fitness that league requires a challenge. At first it was hard for him to keep getting back 10 metres, but he managed it. He became one of the best centres in league when he switched codes, and was still a top player on his return to rugby union.

David Fairleigh had a tremendous season with Saints in 2001. I didn't know much about him before he joined the club as I don't watch much Australian rugby. I knew he had been picked as prop forward of the year while at Newcastle. He's not the biggest of props, but he could run. There are some fat props who just barge in, but he could side-step and pass the ball. He signed to play for the 2002 season, but his shoulder was injured so he only played one season at the club.

Darren Britt played well at St Helens, he took some hammer. He was a great off-loader of the ball. He was a cracking fellow, had some unbelievable stories to tell and was really funny. One year in Lanzarote, he nodded off and the players put plants all around him. They covered him in big palms, he must have woken up thinking he was in the outback. Britto is a top man.

Tommy Martyn was a good footballer, very skilful and had a great boot. He was also an excellent support player and could score tries. He was on my side of the field and I'm glad he was inside me as he could tackle as well. With his ear rings in, I thought he looked like he should have been working at a fairground.

Sean Long is a laugh a minute. I can't say too much. His ability and his fitness levels are so high. He keeps running and running. He's a scrum half and not that big, but he's brave. He has pace and is one of the top men at Saints. I wish I had bought a small house in St Helens when I first joined the club. I wouldn't have moved in, but just used it as a base. Sometimes I would stay in St Helens on Tuesday nights as Ian Millward wanted me to reduce my travelling as it was making my back sore. I used to stay at Sean Long's house. We used to train on Tuesday morning and then Longy and I used to go to the supermarket to get some food for our tea. Longy would buy salmon and pastas and cook me my tea. We used to get some nice snap. He really shocked me - he knew what he was doing. We used to sit in his house, watch Sky and have a brew. I didn't have Sky, so it was a bit of a luxury for me. He used to look after me when I stayed. I think as the weekend came round, it probably wasn't as quiet. It was just as well that I wasn't there. I think things were quieter during the week.

Longy knew who he could have a joke with on match day. With some players, no one would dream of going up to them on match day and saying something stupid to them because they wouldn't acknowledge you. I was a bit of both. I could be alone, but if someone came up to me telling jokes I would listen. Paul Wellens and I used to sit in the physio's room for a home game until it was time to get changed. At the beginning of the season, when it was cold, I used to sit by the radiator in the physio's room to keep warm.

Paul Wellens seemed to come into the first team from nowhere. I can remember him playing for the Academy, because on the first Wednesday of each month at Saints we would have players' awards, voted for by the players after every game. Joynty used to say something and Wello used to scoop quite a few prizes while in the Academy. Soon he was knocking on the door of the first team. He was a stand off when he was coming through and I never really expected him to emerge as a full back. He did though, kept Paul Atcheson out of the side and has never looked back. He's safe under the high ball, his work rate is superb and he brings the ball away well. He's not the quickest of full backs but he's one of the safest. He's one of the top players at the club.

Paul Sculthorpe always gives 110 per cent. His handling ability is second to none and he's another player who has very high fitness levels. His dedication in training is spot on and his physique is good. I think he wears tight t-shirts just to make him look even bigger. He's still quite young and is going to get even better. Scully will keep his concentration and dedication because he's that type of player. When I played, he wasn't the captain, but always had leadership qualities. He had skippered Warrington as a youngster and was always going to captain Saints.

The team celebrating our 2001 World Club Challenge win
(Photo: Bernard Platt)

2001 World Club Challenge: Saluting our fans with Keiron Cunningham and Chris Joynt
(Photo: Bernard Platt)

# 10. End of the (Knowsley) Road

Just before the 2002 Challenge Cup Final, Saints played Bradford away and there was a lot of controversy in the press as we fielded a weakened side and lost 54-22. I was one of the players who didn't play in that game. The club did it again in 2004, again against Bradford. Is it a good thing leaving players out? They are not going to get injured is one way to look at it, but it didn't make a difference for us in 2002 as we were beaten in the final. Hindsight is a wonderful thing though, Ian Millward was obviously thinking about the final and if any coach could do that leading up to a final, I'm sure they would.

Saints had never won at Bradford in Super League. Then came 2002 and our trip to Valley Parade, we blitzed them 50-22 on 16 August and I was among the scorers. It was a warm night and I remember coming off the field absolutely shattered. I knew I'd been in a game but that's true when we play against any of the top sides. It was very quick. We dominated the game particularly in the second half. It was revenge for our earlier defeat.

We ended up winning the Minor Premiership, clinching top spot in the last game of the season against London at Griffin Park. It was a touch-and-go game and I nearly made a mistake that would have cost us the game and top spot.

Before that, I have to describe what happened when Joynty fainted before kick off. It seemed funny. I was rooming with Chris and he was taking some painkillers. Every player takes them for one injury or another so it was nothing unusual for him. He'd been taking these all week, just before the game he had to take another tablet. I remember when he played for Lancashire in the Origin series and had an allergic reaction to a painkiller. He had fainted on that night.

The changing rooms were pretty empty at Griffin Park with most of the players out on the field, there was only a handful of us in there. I was next to Joynty as we were getting changed. The dressing rooms at that ground are really small. Joynty liked to get stripped and rubbed straight away at games; he was always pretty quick whereas I leave it to the last minute to get changed. Joynty was pulling his socks on, nearly ready and I still had my tracksuit on. He turned to me and said: 'I'm roasting, Newy'. I looked at him and he was bright red, I told him he looked as if he was burning up. He said he felt shocking. The next minute I looked at him, he'd changed again; it seemed like David Banner turning into The Hulk. Each time I looked at him the transformation had gone another stage further. He looked as if he had Green Monkeys Disease. His head was growing and his eyes were bulging. His forehead was now bulged out with his cheeks puffed up. He was going all different colours, I did what any decent friend would do, I said: 'F... this, I'm moving' and left him to it. I got out of the way. Claire was strapping someone round the corner and I told her to get round to Joynty as quickly as possible.

By this time, other lads were whispering: 'Bloody hell, look at Joynty'. While I've gone to get Claire, Joynty must have tried to have a walk round and collapsed. Billy Bates was behind him and managed to catch him. Joynty was out. He had to go to hospital and have treatment to calm all the swelling down from his allergic reaction. It was not funny for Chris. The doctors told him that every time he had an allergic reaction it would get worse. The first one at Lancashire must have been mild, but this one was a belter. He was no longer Joynty anymore, he had become a monster. We could put him in one of the *Star Wars* films and save millions on special effects. I wish I'd had a camera with me, I would have said: 'Hold on Joynty before you faint' and captured the moment.

Seriously though, we were worried whether he was going to be alright. The last I saw of him before the game was him being strapped into an ambulance, after being wheeled through the tunnel on a stretcher from the dressing room. After the game, we were all asking about him. Near the end of the game, London put a kick up; I should have gone with my instincts and caught it. Sean Hoppe was behind me though and I thought it's going over my head to him and he will catch it. He thought I was going to catch it and neither of us made a call. I went to catch it and pulled out as I thought I would have gone backwards with it, Hoppe also left it and the ball bounced between us. It rolled and there was a race for it. London thought they had scored, but fortunately it was disallowed. At the time it was racing through my mind that I had cost us the Minor Premiership. After the game, Ian Millward didn't give me a rollicking over the incident. On the long journey home, we were having a beer. He said: 'What about that missed catch Newy?' taking the mickey. I don't think he would have been taking the mickey if we had lost. I got away with it though and it was great to finish top.

The Saints against Sale cross code challenge match in 2003 shocked me. I thought I'd be alright as I'd played a bit of union at school. It was a culture shock. Ray French's son Gary came to the club and gave the forwards a bit of training on rucking and mauling. We didn't know where to stand in defence and struggled with the correct spacing between players. It was like the *Keystone Cops*, everyone was running about like chickens with no heads on. I thought union was pretty slow but it was quicker than I anticipated and that shows their game is getting a bit more professional. Sale are a top side as well and it changed my mind a little bit about union. We killed them at league though, but Longy missed the all important goal that would have made the game a draw. It doesn't matter now, but it did at the time. We wanted to win because they were union and we were league. It was an 'us and them' situation.

In 2003 we were again in the World Club Challenge, this time taking on the Sydney Roosters at the Reebok Stadium, Bolton. I don't think we had a kicking game that day. The first half we defended and scrambled well, but on the night they were better than us. We were struggling for field position, our kicks weren't accurate. The pace of the game was no faster than playing a top four side. We matched them in that department. It wasn't like in 1997 when all the English sides couldn't cope with the pace of the Australian game. We have come on since then and can cope with their pace.

When Saints played UTC in the 2003 Challenge Cup, I didn't fly out with the rest of the team. My auntie died so I went to the funeral. I had to fly out later. I got to Manchester Airport and had something to eat with Adele while I was waiting to go through customs and passport control to the flight. Adele went home and I must have left my passport on the table in the airport cafe. I thought: 'This is a good start' when I realised I didn't have it on me. I was running round the airport like a lunatic, fortunately someone handed it in. One of the airport staff recognised me, came towards me and asked me if I had lost something. I told her my passport, she asked me what my name was, I told her and she gave it to me.

I had to get a flight to Paris and from there I was due to fly to Carcassonne. Someone would pick me up from there and drive me to Perpignan. My form at airports isn't the best, and I thought: 'This could be tricky, but I can do it'. I got to Paris, so far so good.

In Paris, there was an hour and a bit between flights, which was fine because I didn't have a clue where I was going and it is a big airport. I went to the desk of the airline I was travelling with and they sent me to a gate at the other end of the airport. I went down to the gate and thought: 'This seems too easy, it can't be right'. I got right to the gate and it turned out that the flight wasn't headed for Carcassonne but instead was going to Czechoslovakia. If I hadn't asked at the gate I would have boarded it. The woman at the gate said: 'No, wrong, you go that way' in broken English. By this time, they had started boarding on the flight I was supposed to be on. I had to leg it across the airport with my bag full of Saints gear. I just about made it. When I finally got to the team hotel, Claire Mannion was having a coffee in the foyer with the doctor and asked me if everything was alright. 'Alright? I lost my passport and I nearly ended up in Czechoslovakia, yeah, everything's fine!'

I used to have superstitions before a game. I would try and do everything the same way. I think it tailed off as my career went on. When we used to go onto the field, although I'm not religious, I used to say in my head: 'God, please give me a try today'. Sometimes people only talk to God when they want something.

Saints have been involved in so many big matches that are close, but they always end up winning through. The first one to go the other way was the Challenge Cup semi-final against Leeds in 2003. It was a classic game. Darren Smith scored late on and it looked certain that we were through to the final. They got the ball back from a short kick off, and McGuire scored in the corner. Even then I was confident that Sinfield would miss the kick, but he got it and the scores were level. Both sides were out on their feet in extra time, but they took their chance to score and that was it.

Saints employed Mike Sutherland as a nutritionist, he also worked for the Great Britain rugby league side. It turned out that he wasn't qualified, he was actually a fireman. I would have thought that with him working for Great Britain, he would have been checked out properly. We thought we were on a good thing. He was coming to training with tablets for us telling us what was in them. Apparently, it was only multi vitamins he was giving us. We had regular meetings about our diet and our daily intake. He had a file on every player where he would check our weight and our body fat, and set targets for us.

He used to tell us if we had any problems we should ring him. I used to ring him and asked that with my travelling, what could I eat on the way to a game? I used to get bad stomach aches and he told me I wasn't drinking enough water. I started drinking water and my stomach aches went away on game days. I thought: 'This fellow has put me right'. Then we had a meeting and we found out about him. Ian Millward told us what had happened.

I think Stan Wall had his doubts about Sutherland before anybody else. Stan asked questions trying to catch him out and we thought Mike was very defensive. The players were all laughing when we found out the truth. All this time he had been putting out fires and rescuing cats from trees.

On 4 June 2003, Saints announced they wouldn't be keeping me. I was gutted. I remember speaking to Ian Millward during the season and being told that I was his best centre and was playing really well. I thought I'd get a contract for another year. I left it a while then went to see him about it, but he wouldn't give me a straight answer. I then saw on Teletext that Saints were being linked with centres Willie Talau and Nigel Vagana. I went back into see Ian Millward and said: 'Are you going to sign these players?' He told me he would let me know what was happening with my situation in the next couple of weeks. I was called in and I was told by Ian Millward and chief executive Sean McGuire that the club wouldn't be keeping me. I was half expecting it. I was disappointed I hadn't been told this from the beginning. I was a bit down. Leading up to the Wigan game at home on 6 June, Ian came over to me and said if I didn't want to play, I shouldn't play. I told him that I wanted to play and didn't want him to keep me out. I played and I broke my thumb and was out until 15 August for the home fixture against Castleford. Even then, my thumb wasn't right. It wasn't the best end to my time at the club.

I remember at one training session Barry Ward told me that Willie Talau was coming over. I said I knew he had signed to play for Saints from 2004, but Barry told me he was coming over early and was joining the club straight away as Canterbury had released him. I went to Ian Millward and asked why I hadn't been told that Willie was joining us now.

I didn't have any grudges against Willie, he was just doing what any player would do. I had been in the same position as him when I had come to Saints and Paul Loughlin, Bernard Dwyer and Sonny Nickle left the club. I had no qualms with Willie, I was just disappointed with the way the matter had been dealt with by the club. I was very angry and disappointed about it all and after the Castleford game I stormed out of the gym. After the weekend though, the situation calmed down.

I just felt hurt; I had never experienced this before. All through my career, I had clubs chasing me. When a player is older and has had injuries, the club start saying their body isn't up to it anymore. I understand they have got to take that into account and that Ian Millward had to look at the side for the next three years and so on. That's rugby league, players come and go. If a player is too old, the club chucks you out. It makes players sound like a piece of meat and at the end of the day, they are. It comes to everybody but it's not nice.

Bradford fans always booed me, but towards the back end of my career though I could hear supporters from other clubs shout things like: 'You've had your time Newlove', 'You had better hang your boots up' and 'You're looking slow'. I used to think: 'Are they right?' Stuff like that played on my mind. I could either react to comments from the crowd or not. If I reacted, they've won. I didn't like it but I had to deal with it.

My last game at Knowsley Road was against London on 26 September in the play offs. We won 24-6. It was hard saying goodbye to the fans. My son Joe was the mascot that night which was nice. I think Joynty organised that.

It was good to be able to say thanks to the speccies. There was a decent crowd and I got a cheer at the end of the game. Saints chairman Eamonn McManus came onto the pitch and said a few words about me and the year in general to the speccies. All the lads patted me on the back and said well done. Then it hit me that I would be leaving Saints.

My last game for Saints was at Wigan in the play-offs. I scored but it was a disappointment as we got trounced 40-24. I don't think I played well. One of the worst moments in my career was when I kicked the ball and Wigan went the full length of the pitch and scored. It was nice to get a try, but the game itself wasn't really a classic memory for me.

It was a sad day. It ended Saints' season and we got a big rollicking after the game from Ian Millward. I said my goodbyes and that was it.

## Sean Long played alongside Paul at St Helens

"It was brilliant playing in the same side as Paul. When I first joined the club, I was only 21 and Paul was one of the legend-type players there. Everyone knew about Newy. He was very down-to-earth, laidback and chilled out off the field with a very dry sense of humour. On the field, he could turn a game on its head when nothing much was happening or we were struggling to break a defence down. Newy didn't touch the ball that often, but when he did, he could make a break from anywhere.

A memory that stands out for me about Paul is a game we played against Warrington and Kohe Love was playing opposite Newy. Every time Newy got the ball, he skinned Kohe Love, who couldn't lay a finger on him. By the end of the game they swapped Kohe Love to the other side of the field because he couldn't handle Paul's step and his power.

Another great memory of him is in the 2002 Grand Final against Bradford. It was 18-18 and we got the ball on our own line. Tony Stewart made a break on the left hand side. We were walking our way towards the posts. Newy just came on to a pass and took us right to the posts. That showed his experience, he knew the script, no-one said we were going for a drop goal, he just knew what to do. After one more drive towards the posts, I got the drop goal and that won us the game.

Newy was pretty quiet in the dressing room. I knew him a bit better than the other lads, so I'd go and have a chat with him. He would sit on his own generally. He didn't mix words very often, he didn't speak much but when he did, everyone listened and understood what he was saying.

He used to wear these undies, he would wear two pairs of underpants before every game. He had a lucky pair and another pair for everyday use. By the time he left St Helens, they were absolutely filthy. He might have washed them. The years had obviously taken their toll.

During his last year at the club, the travel was taking its toll on him. I said to him that I lived on my own and he could come and stay at my place anytime he wanted. We would train and with it being early in the week, I wouldn't have much food in so we would go to the supermarket. He would be buying salmon, fresh veg and sauce. We'd go home and cook our tea. He would drink about 45 million brews after his feed. I'm not joking, the kettle was always on all night. It was always me who had to make the brews. He would be lying on the couch, watching telly and ordering biscuits. Newy was good fun.

He's as tight as a cramp as well! I speak to him quite often, he's chilled out. He called it a day on his career at the right time because I think we had the best of him."

## Chris Joynt was Paul's skipper at St Helens

Newy and I played alongside each other at international level. We met around 1993 playing in France, probably on one of my first Great Britain appearances. From that day, we've always been good friends. When Saints had the opportunity to sign him, it was very pleasing as he was a world class player who could only add to the team's strength. He joined us at the pomp of his career and Paul, Sully and I formed a deadly partnership down the left flank.

He was very quiet in the dressing room and kept to himself. Every player is different; we wouldn't hear two words from Newy throughout the whole build up towards a game. We were lucky to get two words out him on the pitch as well.

Nobody gave us a chance to beat Brisbane in the 2001 World Club Challenge and that made our win even better. One of the major factors in our win was the try I scored after Newy broke through. He made a break down the left flank and I was on his inside to take his pass. Mind you, it wasn't the best pass, I had to take it one handed as the ball was going away from me. We got the result that we wanted and I'm sure it's something that Newy and I will talk about in years to come, as will a lot of Saints supporters.

All the stories about him being afraid of flying and not wanting to tour are rubbish. He's just a lad who keeps to himself and when has done a lot in his career. He has a wicked sense of humour, he's a very dry, funny bloke but we had to draw that out of him. All the lads enjoyed his company because of the way he acted.

It's funny, but when we went to Cardiff in 2004 for the Cup Final, the big question was: 'Who's Joynty going to room with now Newy's gone?' Paul and I always roomed together. As I said, Newy doesn't talk much and I can be a stubborn so-and-so. There was one instance where we were both lying on our beds, not the same bed I must add! We were watching television and my mobile phone went off. I checked it and Newy had sent me a text message: 'Put the kettle on'. I promptly sent one back telling him where to go and that he should put the kettle on. Neither of us would make the brew and all this happened without a word being spoken.

I could fill a chapter about his dog. Newy asked me at training: 'Would I look after his dog while an extension was being built at his house?' I said 'no problem'.

Newy came to training soon after that with this dog and every possession it had ever owned in the back of his car. I looked at it and thought: 'What am I going to do with this?' I hadn't made any plans about where it was going to live. I was living at my parents at the time. My mum must have been thinking: 'Our Chris is getting dafter as he's getting older; he's brought a Staffordshire Bull home with him from training'. I explained that it was Newy's dog and we only had it for a month. A week later in training, Newy said to me 'Guess what Joynty, six weeks before my bricks even arrive for the extension'. I ran another half lap or so and said: 'We've only got the dog for a month'.

Five years on, we've still got it. At first, we had a little deal going, he had told me that it was going to cost £4 a day to keep the dog in kennels so I said I would charge £2.50 a day. That soon went out of the window because it cost him too much. It had to go to the vet and the bill was around £100 so I ended up paying the bill. A couple of days later, Newy brought me its registration papers so that I became its owner and was liable for all the costs, vet bills and so on. My dad is convinced that it killed someone in Yorkshire and needed to get out of the area as quickly as possible and where better to take it than our house. When Newy's extension was finally built I asked Paul about taking the dog back and got the reply: 'We're not having it chewing our house up'.

We were in Lanzarote for warm weather training and Ian Millward, Newy and I went out one afternoon. We had trained hard throughout the week and were allowed to go out that afternoon for a few beers. On the way home in the taxi, Newy farted. The place in Lanzarote where we were staying was in the middle of nowhere. The taxi driver jumped out, opened all the doors and started shouting 'no farto, no farto'. He was going to drop us off because they class breaking wind as ignorant. We were in the middle of nowhere with this taxi driver going berserk. We had to talk him round to take us back to where we were staying. He was maintaining that we were pigs and it took a while to reason with him. Newy wouldn't own up to farting, but it was definitely him. On the same trip Newy and I were rooming together and he had a clock he had been given at Featherstone for getting into the 1992 Great Britain touring side. Training was very hard, and after lunch we would generally go to bed for a couple of hours, then get up for the afternoon training stint. Newy was very proud of this clock and insisted it had never lost a second. Just as he was saying that there was a knock on the door. It was Stan Wall telling us that it was 3.15pm and we were late for training. Newy said: 'It can't be, my clock says it's quarter to and this clock has never lost a second'. Anyway the clock which never lost a second was half an hour slow and we had to go to training late. Millward fined us so they could all have a few drinks on us and with the lads knowing we're both tight bastards, it made it even sweeter for everybody."

Playing for Great Britain against New Zealand
(Photo: David Williams)

Playing for England against Australia in the 1995 World Cup
(Photo: David Williams)

125

Playing for Castleford
(Photo: David Williams)

# 11. Jungle foot

After leaving Saints I told Peter Fox that I would like to sign for Hull. Peter was due to be on a golfing weekend with Shaun McRae and said he would speak to him then.  Something happened and Peter didn't go on the golfing weekend, so he didn't have chance to speak to McRae. Peter went to Castleford and approached Graham Steadman. They agreed the deal for me to go to the club. It was only 15 minutes down the road for me which suited me after all my travelling to St Helens. I felt sorry for Graham when he was later sacked as coach. I don't think how the team performed was his fault, and I hope he gets back into the game.

The Castleford lads were great with me, they have kept in touch with me even though I only played five games for them. I have nothing but praise for everyone connected with the Castleford club. I scored my one and only try for them in my home debut against London. It was a 70 metre interception try. I could see it coming off when London's scrum half Dennis Moran got the ball, and I intercepted his pass. I still had enough pace left to score.

A foot injury ended my career. My foot was alright in training, but training and playing are two different things. In training I could just ease back on the injury. It just wouldn't stand up to the 100 per cent effort in a game. I had the injury towards the back end of my time at St Helens, but I never thought anything of it then. After a game, my foot was sore the next day. I started pre-season training at Castleford and at first I felt fine. I was doing weights, running and track work without a problem. Then gradually after every session my foot was more and more sore. One day it got to the point where I couldn't run. Ten minutes jogging and that would be it.

I played in a friendly at Huddersfield. I think the board wanted me to play. I told Jonesy the Castleford physio that I was not fit to play. He agreed, but said 'just see what you can do'. As I was warming up, I knew my foot had gone. I played for 35 minutes and I was in agony. I don't know how I did it. There was the possibility that it could snap, so that was playing on my mind too.

I don't know exactly how I got the injury. It may just have been wear and tear. It's the same foot as my Achilles injury so that has to be taken into account. Maybe that has put more pressure on it.

Fair play to Jonesy, he was very good with me and did everything that he could to get my foot right.

He said he has seen this type of injury before and that Barrie Jon Mather had experienced the same problem, but his cleared up. Jonesy told me that the injury would heal in time. He told me I would be sent for lipotripsy - a machine that helps the injury. I was booked in to be treated by this big machine down in Devon. Until my appointment I was having a little machine used on the injury. It wasn't as powerful as the one in Devon but it made a start on the injury. I had to visit a physio in Leeds for the smaller machine. It was just like a little box and at the end of it was a sort of pneumatic drill that went in and out really quickly. They put it on my tendon and knocked hell out of it.

When UTC travelled to play Castleford in the Challenge Cup I went to Devon to have the big machine used on my foot. I went to the hospital and the machine had broken down, so I travelled back home the next day. Three days later, I was booked in again. The big machine hurt a lot more than the little one, it felt like it was needles going into my foot. I just had to grin and bear it, but ended up having to chew on the pillow. They told me that the treatment should clear up my injury, and to give it six weeks until I started running again.

My first game was at Hull and I still had to have an injection to be able to play. The same thing happened in the next three games. I had a painkilling injection to numb my foot; it worked until towards the end of the second half when I would be subbed.

It was a relief to retire. I wasn't doing myself justice as my foot was causing me a lot of problems. I was letting myself and the club down as I couldn't perform. I had a meeting with the club's new coach Gary Mercer and told him that I couldn't give him 100 per cent. He had realised I was struggling with my foot so had played me, then rested me. He said he wanted me to play at home against Salford on 23 May 2004 as it was a Grand Final type of game for them.

I wasn't right, it was the first time that season that I played without an injection. I wanted to see how long it lasted, but I didn't last long. There was no mobility in my foot. I hobbled in at half time and Gary asked how I was feeling. I told him I would be alright to go back out. As soon as I sat down I thought: 'What have I just said there?' After he had given his team talk I went to him and told him that it wasn't alright and that I was struggling. I went back on in the second half, but he took me off after 10 minutes. That was my last game and we lost 36-32. I had to hold my hands up after the game, be realistic and say that it just wasn't working.

The next day I went to the club to see Gary Mercer and told him I was going to retire. Foxy rang the chief executive Richard Wright. We came to an agreement. I could have just sat it out, playing 40 minutes one game then sat two or three games out while picking up my contract money, but I didn't want to do that to Castleford. It was no good to me or the club. I knew that they needed to start winning games quickly and that the money saved on not having to pay me could go towards bringing in new players. It wasn't fair on the supporters either; they paid their money and deserved to see the best team out on the field. I couldn't give them 100 per cent, so all round it was best if I called it a day. My foot has got a bit better since retiring but it was never going to be 100 per cent for rugby league again.

Retiring has obviously had a big impact on my life. During the lead up to a game, I didn't want to go anywhere. I just liked to be on my own. It could be a bit hard for my son Joe when he wanted me to play cricket or run round the garden with him and I had to say no because I was playing that weekend.

I spoke to former Saints forward Barry Ward who retired in 2003 and asked him if he missed the game and he said he doesn't. A lot of former players I've spoken to say the same. I know I won't miss it. It was a job at the end of the day. One thing is that when I stopped being a professional sportsman, my car insurance shot down. That's a bonus.

One thing I will miss is the banter in the changing rooms. I can't tell you half the stuff that goes on, but it's entertaining and there are still some characters about. I always enjoyed having a beer after training or after a game with my mates. Going out after a big win when you're all buzzing is also fun. And some players are a bit thicker than others, we could take the mickey out of them because they didn't catch on as quickly.

I was speaking to Chris Joynt recently and told him I might get over to see a few Saints games. I have no ties at weekends now as I'm not playing, so I could nip to see Saints on a Friday night and go out with the lads afterwards.

I went on a coaching course as I thought I might as well get the qualification. I booked on it with Joynty. Ray Unsworth ran it at Bolton for two days. Also there were Paul Sculthorpe, Paul Deacon,

Paul Anderson, Andy Farrell, Alan Hunte, Steve Blakeley, Barrie McDermott and a few guys from the National League such as Graham Hallas and Paul Harrison. Various people came and gave us talks. Ray said to us that he wasn't going to stand in front of us and try and teach us how to coach rugby league as we had all played at international level or a high standard. He said: 'What was the point of him trying to tell us what to do'. Instead they were going to give us useful information on a variety of topics. They had a psychologist come to talk to us, then a fitness guy. The fitness expert thought we were doing a 90 minute exam. He was talking to us about heart rates and said: 'When you do your test...' and Andy Farrell piped up with: 'There's no effing test in here lad', which made everyone laugh. It was like a two day seminar and technically I am a qualified rugby league coach who could coach up to international level.

# 12. The future

I have been described as one of the best players of my generation, but I don't see myself like that. It is kind and I feel good about people saying that, but deep down I think: 'Am I really?' I think I was just a normal player. I must have been doing something right I suppose. Wherever I've been, I used to get letters from people from all over the place, not just Lancashire and Yorkshire, but also from people down south, Birmingham and so on. People watch rugby league down there and I used to think: 'Bloody hell, they want my autograph' or whatever. I may not be so well known down there, but there were people who used to write to me.

I was in a pub in York recently and a French rugby league side were there for a tournament. They recognised me and bought me a couple of pints which was nice. Sometimes I don't realise how much people react to what I have done.

I think I underestimate myself at times. Peter Fox once told me that if I had stayed at Featherstone, people would see me as just a local lad, slap me on the back and say that I'd done well. But when a player moves to a bigger club people see them as more of a star. I was treated better as a result, so Foxy was right.

I've always said that when I retired and people are sitting round in a pub in St Helens talking about rugby league, if my name comes up in conversation and they say: 'He was a good player' then I think I've done  my job. That's what they used to say about my dad and I think if I'm remembered in the game in a similar way that is something special. I remember Andy Northey saying that when he retired he would sit in the pub as an old man in his Wembley suit saying: 'I played for Saints you know'. Andy is a good lad, maybe he was winding me up.

I'd say one of my main strengths as a player was my left foot step. Everybody knew I had it, but they still had to stop it. I also think I had a good pair of hands. I could always catch, an ability some players don't have, and I could also pass. I also felt I had good balance, if I got a knock or a hit I could ride it without breaking my stride.

I'm pleased to be in the top 20 British try scorers of all time. I was a try scorer throughout my career, I loved scoring tries and to be in that all-time list is amazing. It's hard to get in there, but I wish I was in the top 10. I hope I stay there for some years.

I don't know if I could pick a best moment of my career. I certainly enjoyed my game for Yorkshire. My first Wembley Challenge Cup Final was great. Early in my career, playing against Castleford for Featherstone and scoring was a superb feeling. I've been lucky in that I have had so many special moments in my career. It's hard to pick out particular moments; every match has its own points I remember.

As for the sport itself, is rugby league going anywhere? I think it's mainly a northern sport. UTC are set to come in from France, but they already tried it with Paris St Germain and that didn't work. Is there enough money in the game? If Sky Television pulled out, and their income was lost, the sport would be in serious trouble. The sport has improved in my time though.

As for hobbies, I play a bit of golf and go fishing with Smiggy. He really likes it, I just do it to get out and have a sit in the sun. I am interested in fishing though. I like outdoor activities such as gardening. For pets, we have ducks at the bottom of the garden; we used to have chickens, but the fox took them. My wife has a horse and the kids have got guinea pigs. I'm not really one for pets, but it's like anything else, the kids say they'll look after their pets and I end up doing it all. I was the same at their age.

I also like cooking. All the cookery programmes on television have made it more fashionable. I like watching Ainsley Harriett, I'm thinking of doing a cookery course. I've made some good stuff, I like to have people round and cook for them. We used to have Christmas dinner at Adele's mum's house, but we have it at our house now. All the family like it because I make a special effort and do something fancy. As it is Christmas, I like to spike it up and put a bit of a show on rather than just the normal roast.

It's difficult because Adele's dad is just a roast beef and potato man; he likes things to be plain and bland. I do a separate dish for him by putting some braising steak under the grill. Yorkshire pudding is as far as he will go.

On television, I like *Emmerdale*. I've dropped off a bit, it's not the same without the Dingles. They used to make me laugh, without Butch and co it's changed. That programme used to be my top priority, now I'll only watch it if I'm not doing anything else. As well as soaps, I enjoy documentaries and comedy shows. I like watching films especially any with Clint Eastwood or John Wayne.

I'm not a big lover of music. I listen to Radio Two in the car. I used to like listening to Terry Wogan in the morning on the way to

St Helens. I think Radio Two plays better music than Radio One. I don't like all this modern stuff because I don't know what they're on about half the time. It's very rare I go out and buy a CD.

A vocal moment that stands out is when the Saints lads would sing 'I love Newlove' to the tune of Gary Glitter's *I Love You Love Me*. When we were out and they had a couple of drinks, it would always get a rendition. Darren Albert used to sing it a lot to take the mickey. I used to tell him to shut up.

Another singing opportunity was when Johnny Vegas did a CD with Mungo Jerry for Joynty's testimonial. We all went down to a studio in St Helens. It was only a little room up some stairs round the back of the Town Hall. I wasn't going to go as it was after a training session and with my drive back over the Pennines, it would have made me late home. I didn't think my vocal talents would be missed as all the other lads were there. Anyway, Joynty asked me to come, so I went along. I'm glad I did as it was another interesting experience. All we had to do was sing the chorus. Mungo wasn't there, he did his bit in another studio and then they put it all together.

Now my rugby league career has come to an end, I'm coming to another crossroads in my life. What do I do with myself after all this time in rugby league? I'll have to sit down and think about it, it's scary really because all I've known has been rugby league. When I left school, I could have got a trade, but I went into playing rugby instead. I must admit that the game was still part-time when I started, so I suppose I could have got a trade. There was training on Tuesday and Thursday nights; and we played on Sunday so I could have done something else. But I stuck to what I knew. I didn't really want to work, I just thought: 'I can play rugby, it's easy and I'm getting paid for it.' I'm glad I stuck to sport.

Now I have retired from playing, I think I will fade out of the public eye. It would be nice to make the occasional appearance on Sky or whatever, but I don't think I have the confidence to go on and develop that area of work. I think my limit would be returning to Knowsley Road to give the crowd a wave.

I would like to coach at Academy level as there is less pressure there. A job going into schools and teaching basic skills to kids, as a development officer would suit me. We did a lot of that work at Saints, doing little drills with kids. I've done it in my home area as well. If anything like that came up I'd be very interested. I think it is something clubs should do a lot more. It is important to get into the schools and get kids interested in the game. The best players could go to their local club. Even if they only get one first team player out of 100 that player might become a good one.

I've made no particular plans for the future, I'm happy just strolling along. Having said that, I have no money coming in, so I must do some work outside the game for the first time in my life. I've got to do my bit.

Some people may be surprised that I have written a book. I just thought that not many people can say that they have written a book. I don't know if people will like it but I hope they will. When I was first approached to do it, I thought it was Barry Ward taking the mickey. This is because my co-writer was living in Australia at the time and the letter came from there. I went on the internet to see if I could find out a bit more information and thought: 'Hang on, it might be alright' and it went on from there. I did have moments where I thought: 'Who wants to read what I've done? All I've done is sat on the settee, watched telly and played a bit of rugby league'.

I would like to thank fans for their support throughout my career. Not just in St Helens, but the people in Featherstone, Bradford and Castleford too, and those down south who wrote to me. Thanks to all the supporters who encouraged me. It was a good 16 years.

Presenting Leeds Rhinos' Danny McGuire with a plate
in recognition of his achievement in breaking my record
for tries scored in a Super League season.
(Photo: David Williams)

# Appendix: Statistics and records

## International and representative appearances

### Great Britain Tests:

| 1989: | New Zealand (sub) | Old Trafford | Lost 16-24 | |
| | New Zealand | Elland Road | Won 26-6 | |
| | New Zealand (WC) | Wigan | Won 10-6 | |
| 1991: | Papua New Guinea (WC) | Wigan | Won 56-4 | **1t** |
| 1992: | Papua New Guinea (sub) | Port Moresby | Won 20-14 | |
| | Australia | Sydney | Lost 6-22 | |
| | Australia | Melbourne | Won 33-10 | **1t** |
| | Australia | Brisbane | Lost 10-16 | |
| | New Zealand (sub) | Auckland | Won 19-16 | |
| 1993: | France | Leeds | Won 72-6 | **3t** |
| | New Zealand | Wembley | Won 17-0 | |
| | New Zealand | Wigan | Won 29-12 | **1t** |
| | New Zealand | Leeds | Won 29-10 | |
| 1994: | France | Carcassonne | Won 12-4 | **1t** |
| | Australia (sub) | Old Trafford | Lost 8-38 | **1t** |
| | Australia | Elland Road | Lost 4-23 | |
| 1997: | Australia (SL) | Wembley | Lost 14-38 | |
| | Australia (SL) | Old Trafford | Won 20-12 | |
| | Australia (SL) | Elland Road | Lost 20-37 | |
| 1998: | New Zealand | Huddersfield | Lost 16-22 | **1t** |

**Summary:** Won 12. Lost 8. 9 tries.

### Great Britain matches on tour:

| 1992: | Highlands Zone (PNG) | Goroka | Won 24-15 | |
| 1992: | Islands Zone (PNG) | Rabaul | Won 38-20 | |
| 1992: | Queensland Res (sub) | Townsville | Won 14-10 | |
| 1992: | Canberra | Canberra | Won 24-12 | **1t** |
| 1992: | Paramatta | Paramatta | Lost 16-22 | |
| 1992: | Auckland | Auckland | Won 14-8 | |
| 1992: | Canterbury | Christchurch | Won 17-6 | **1t** |

**Summary:** Won 6. Lost 1. 2 tries.

### England:

| 1992: | Wales | Swansea | Won 36-11 | **1t** |
| 1995: | Wales | Cardiff | Lost 16-18 | |
| | Australia (WC) | Wembley | Won 20-16 | **1t** |
| | Fiji (WC) | Wigan | Won 46-0 | **1t** |
| | Wales (WC Semi-Final) | Old Trafford | Won 25-10 | **1t** |
| | Australia (WC Final) | Wembley | Lost 8-16 | **1t** |
| 1996: | France | Gateshead | Won 73-6 | **2t** |

**Summary:** Won 5. Lost 2. 7 tries.

(WC: World Cup. SL: Super League.)

## Great Britain under-21 appearances:

| 1989 | France | Leeds | Won 30-0 | **1t, 1g** |
|------|--------|-------|----------|-----------|
| 1989 | France | Carpentras | Lost 8-16 | **2g** |
| 1990 | France | Villeneuve | Won 22-0 | |
| 1990 | France | Doncaster | Won 20-6 | **1t** |
| 1991 | France | Limoux | Won 48-2 | |
| 1991 | Papua New Guinea | Leeds | Won 58-0 | **2t** |
| 1992 | France | Halifax | Won 56-2 | |
| 1992 | France | Albi | Won 34-2 | |

**Summary:** Won 7. Lost 1. 4 tries. 3 goals.

## Yorkshire

| 1989 | Lancashire | Wigan | Won 56-12 | **2t** |
|------|------------|-------|-----------|--------|

## Honours and milestones

- Young Player of the Year: 1988-89.
- Top Try Scorer: 1992-93, 1996.
- Division Two Player of the Year: 1992-93.
- Most expensive player – transfer deal valued at £500,000 from Bradford to St Helens in 1995.
- Youngest Great Britain international: 1989.
- Featherstone Rovers record try scorer in a season – 48 in 1992-93.
- Record holder most tries in Super League season: 28 in 1996 (until 2004)
- Record holder scoring a try in successive games in Super League – 9 in 1996 (still joint holder)

### Club honours

| Club | Season | Honours |
|------|--------|---------|
| Featherstone | 1989-90 | Yorkshire Cup runners up |
| Featherstone | 1992-93 | *Division Two Champions, Divisional Premiership winners* |
| St Helens | 1995-96 | Regal Trophy runners up |
| St Helens | 1996 | *Challenge Cup winners, Super League winners,* Premiership runners up |
| St Helens | 1997 | *Challenge Cup winners,* Premiership runners up |
| St Helens | 1999 | *Super League winners* |
| St Helens | 2000 | *Super League winners,* World Club Challenge runners up |
| St Helens | 2001 | *World Club Challenge winners, Challenge Cup winners* |
| St Helens | 2002 | *Super League winners,* Challenge Cup runners up |
| St Helens | 2003 | World Club Challenge runners up |

## Summary:

**Super League:** Winners: 4.
**Challenge Cup:** Winners: 3. Runners up: 1
**World Club Challenge:** Winners: 1. Runners up: 2.
**Premiership:** Runners up: 2.
**Regal Trophy:** Runners up 1.
**Yorkshire Cup:** Runners up 1.
**Division Two:** Winners 1.
**Divisional Premiership:** Winners 1.

## Statistics

| Season | Team | App | Tries | Goals | DG | Pts |
|---|---|---|---|---|---|---|
| 1988-89 | Featherstone | 30 | 18 | 9 | 0 | 90 |
| 1989-90 | Featherstone | 30 | 18 | 0 | 0 | 72 |
| 1990-91 | Featherstone | 23 | 13 | 0 | 0 | 52 |
| 1991-92 | Featherstone | 32 | 25 | 0 | 0 | 100 |
| 1992-93 | Featherstone | 35 | 48 | 0 | 0 | 192 |
| 1993-94 | Bradford | 34 + 2 | 35 | 0 | 0 | 140 |
| 1994-95 | Bradford | 27 + 1 | 25 | 0 | 0 | 100 |
| 1995-96 | Bradford | 6 | 6 | 0 | 0 | 24 |
| 1995-96 | St Helens | 5 | 3 | 0 | 0 | 12 |
| 1996 | St Helens | 27 | 36 | 0 | 0 | 144 |
| 1997 | St Helens | 30 | 19 | 0 | 0 | 76 |
| 1998 | St Helens | 28 | 19 | 0 | 0 | 76 |
| 1999 | St Helens | 29 | 19 | 0 | 0 | 76 |
| 2000 | St Helens | 16 | 8 | 0 | 0 | 32 |
| 2001 | St Helens | 21 | 15 | 0 | 0 | 60 |
| 2002 | St Helens | 27 | 7 | 0 | 0 | 28 |
| 2003 | St Helens | 24 | 8 | 0 | 0 | 32 |
| 2004 | Castleford | 5 | 1 | 0 | 0 | 4 |
| 1989 - 1998 | Great Britain | 16 + 4 | 9 | 0 | 0 | 36 |
| 1992 -1996 | England | 7 | 7 | 0 | 0 | 28 |
| 1989 -1992 | Great Britain u-21 | 8 | 4 | 0 | 0 | 16 |
| 1989-90 | Yorkshire | 1 | 2 | 0 | 0 | 4 |
| 1992 | Great Britain touring team | 6 +1 | 2 | 0 | 0 | 8 |
| **Totals** | | 467 | 347 | 9 | 0 | 1,402 |

## Club league records

| Season | Team | Div | Pl | W | D | L | Pts | Position |
|---|---|---|---|---|---|---|---|---|
| 1988-89 | Featherstone | One | 26 | 13 | 1 | 12 | 27 | 6 |
| 1989-90 | Featherstone | One | 26 | 10 | 0 | 16 | 20 | 10 |
| 1990-91 | Featherstone | One | 26 | 12 | 1 | 3 | 25 | 8 |
| 1991-92 | Featherstone | One | 26 | 11 | 0 | 15 | 22 | 13 (R) |
| 1992-93 | Featherstone | Two | 28 | 24 | 1 | 3 | 49 | 1 (P) |
| 1993-94 | Bradford | One | 30 | 23 | 0 | 7 | 46 | 2 |
| 1994-95 | Bradford | One | 30 | 17 | 1 | 12 | 35 | 7 |
| 1995-96 | Bradford * | Cent | 20 | 8 | 0 | 12 | 16 | 7 |
| 1995-96 | St Helens * | Cent | 20 | 12 | 0 | 8 | 24 | 4 |
| 1996 | St Helens | SL | 22 | 20 | 0 | 2 | 40 | 1 |
| 1997 | St Helens | SL | 22 | 14 | 1 | 7 | 29 | 3 |
| 1998 | St Helens | SL | 23 | 14 | 1 | 8 | 29 | 4 |
| 1999 | St Helens | SL | 30 | 23 | 0 | 7 | 46 | 2 |
| 2000 | St Helens | SL | 28 | 23 | 0 | 5 | 46 | 2 |
| 2001 | St Helens | SL | 28 | 17 | 2 | 9 | 36 | 4 |
| 2002 | St Helens | SL | 28 | 23 | 0 | 5 | 46 | 1 |
| 2003 | St Helens ** | SL | 28 | 16 | 1 | 11 | 31 | 4 |
| 2004 | Castleford * | SL | 28 | 6 | 0 | 22 | 12 | 14 (R) |

\*   Paul Newlove only played part of season.

\*\* Two points deducted for salary cap breach in 2002.

## Tries scored against different clubs

| | |
|---|---|
| Castleford | 31 |
| Leeds | 28 |
| Halifax | 22 |
| Oldham | 21 |
| Warrington | 19 |
| Sheffield Eagles | 17 |
| London | 16 |
| Salford | 15 |
| Bramley | 13 |
| Hull | 12 |
| Widnes | 11 |
| Whitehaven | 11 |
| Bradford | 11 |
| Huddersfield | 9 |
| Workington | 8 |
| St Helens | 8 |
| Leigh | 8 |
| Wakefield | 7 |
| Rochdale | 7 |
| Swinton | 5 |
| Wigan | 4 |
| Hunslet | 4 |
| Doncaster | 4 |
| Dewsbury | 4 |
| Barrow | 4 |
| Paris | 3 |
| Keighley | 3 |
| Hull KR | 3 |
| Gateshead | 3 |
| Carlisle | 3 |
| Batley | 3 |
| York | 2 |
| Featherstone | 2 |
| Cronulla | 1 |

### Four tries in a club match:
*Featherstone R:* 1992-93: Bramley (h).
*Bradford N:* 1993-94: Barrow (a).

### Three tries in a club match:
*Featherstone R:* 1989-90: Leigh (h).
1991-92: Batley (a).
1992-93: London C (h), Oldham (h), Bramley (h), Rochdale H (h), Bramley (a)
*Bradford N:* 1993-94: Leeds (a), Leeds (h).
1994-95: Oldham (h), Doncaster (h).
1995-96: Sheffield Eagles (h).
*St Helens:* 1996: Castleford (a), Workington (a), Halifax (a), Oldham (h).
1997: Hull (h).

# From Great Broughton to Great Britain
## *Peter Gorley – Rugby League Forward*
## By Peter Cropper

**Peter Gorley** was one of the outstanding second-row forwards of his generation. He is also one of the best Cumbrian rugby league players of the last 30 years. This book covers his complete rugby league career, including: his days in the amateur game; turning professional with **Workington Town,** including playing in three Lancashire Cup Finals; playing for **St Helens**, including winning the Lancashire Cup and Premiership and his representative career – playing for Great Britain, England and Cumbria.

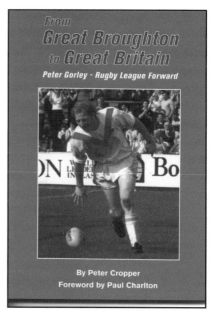

The book recalls great battles on the pitch, and an era when rugby league was still played part-time even at the top level.

**Published in April 2004 at £9.95.**
**ISBN: 1903659-16-7.**

**Special offer to readers of this book: Order for £9.00 post free from London League Publications Ltd, PO Box 10441, London E14 8WR (Cheques to London League Publications Ltd). Available at full price on our website www.llpshop.co.uk or from bookshops**

# Beyond the heartlands
## The history of the Rugby League Conference
### By Julian Harrison

Since its inception as the Summer Conference League in 1997, the Rugby League Conference has played a major role in spreading Rugby League throughout England and Wales, and making it a truly national sport. This is the inside story of the new League's development, by one of its founders and former full-time administrator.

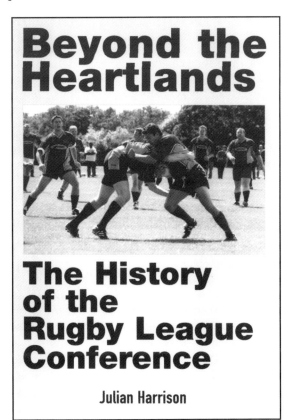

**Published in October 2004 at £12.95.**
**ISBN: 1903659-17-5**

**Order post free from London League Publications Ltd, PO Box 10441, London E14 8WR, or for credit card orders via our website: www.llpshop.co.uk**
**Also available in bookshops.**

# Give it to Kelly!
## A Rugby League Saga
## By John D. Vose

This new rugby league saga features the mythical Lancashire team from the 1930s, Bramfield Rovers, and their ongoing struggles to survive.

It recalls Lancashire in the 1930s. Dole queues, pawnbrokers' shops beneath the sign of the three brass balls, factory chimneys belching out smoke, the piercing shriek of the mill hooter summoning folk to a day's work. But on Saturday, there was rest from hard toil and... Rugby... fast, hard-tackling Rugby League... the northern working class game. Perhaps Rochdale were playing at home to Saints or Oldham hosting Hull Kingston Rovers at Watersheddings... in these towns Rugby League was king. In Bramfield, it was the same.

Bramfield Rovers have reached an all-time low. Bottom of the league and on the verge of bankruptcy. Is the end in sight? When club scout Stanley Keighley is sent on a scouting mission to a posh North Yorkshire Rugby Union club and is chased away by an outraged Colonel's Afghan hounds, he sets off a series of bizarre events.

Readers will discover:

- A wizard centre with a double-barrelled name;
- A Russian spy masquerading as a belly dancer from Heckmondwike on the run from Captain Montague-Morency of MI6;
- A light-fingered, smooth-talking Australian: a try-scoring rugby genius who can streak past defenders, beguile Lancashire barmaids and daughters of the aristocracy with equal aplomb, and then set the police forces of Yorkshire and Lancashire hot on his trail; and
- How undertaker-cum-scout Stanley Keighley, the man who once signed a player with a wooden leg, learns to regret signing the 'Wizard of Oz' and makes club chairman Joshua Hepplethwaite want to bury the boozy undertaker in one of his own coffins.

**Published in October 2003 at £8.95. ISBN: 1903659-11-6**

**Special offer for readers of this book: Order for £5.00 from London League Publications Ltd, PO Box 10441, London E14 8WR (Cheques payable to London League Publications Ltd)**

**The Rugby League magazine for all the game's supporters**

**Published twice a year**

- Analysis of current issues

- Features covering all sections of Rugby League

- History of the game including 'My Great Match' in each edition

- Book Reviews

- Obituaries

- And our cartoon Grubber

**£2.50 per issue, or a four issue subscription for £9.00**

**Order from:**
**London League Publications Ltd, PO Box 10441, London E14 8WR**
**or order via our website: www.llpshop.co.uk**

For details of all our Rugby League books
and publications, and a free catalogue,
write to:


# London League Publications Ltd
# PO Box 10441
# London E14 8WR


Or


Visit our website:


# www.llpshop.co.uk

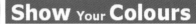
146